PRAYERS
that avail much®

First Blessings for Your Child

GERMAINE COPELAND

Prayers That Avail Much®
First Blessings for Your Child by Germaine Copeland
Published by Creation House
A part of Strang Communications Company
600 Rinehart Road
Lake Mary, Florida 32746
www.creationhouse.com

Cover and interior design by Pat Theriault

Library of Congress Catalog Card Number: 00-111452
International Standard Book Number: 0-88419-740-9

1 2 3 4 5 6 7 8 Berryville 8 7 6 5 4 3 2 1
Printed in the United States of America

I dedicate this book to our grandchildren:
Matthew, Joseph, Rachel, Leah,
Martha Jean,
Chandler Grace and Griffin,
and to
future generations.
May your good deeds glow for all to see.

Thank you, Donna Walker,
for your valuable assistance in writing and rewriting.
Thank you, Rick Nash, for your vision for this
book; Renee Deloria for your editing; and the other
staff members of Creation House for your
dedicated professionalism.

Once again, I owe a debt of gratitude to the
Word Ministries intercessors that have prayed for
this publication. May you be liberally rewarded
and your families blessed.

I am ever grateful to my parents,
Rev. A. H. "Buck" Griffin and
Donnis Brock Griffin (now in heaven),
who taught me to pray without ceasing.

Contents

Introduction

Welcome to *Prayers That Avail Much® First Blessings for Your Child.* Words may be the most powerful force in our universe.

Words shape our destiny and the destinies of our children. Parents, you have the opportunity to write the first chapter of a new book. The blessings that you read to your child from this book will pave the way for him or her to know the God of creation—the God who loves him, chose him and planned his life before the foundation of the world.

My parents were the very first people I heard utter a prayer. We prayed on bended knee in the morning and evening. We listened to our mother and father pray before praying the Lord's Prayer together. My father closed each night's prayer with, "Lord, we thank You for the angels who are encamped round about our home to watch over and protect us." We went to bed comforted and unafraid.

Often the Holy Spirit reminds me of the Word that was either read to me or prayed for me. Our children will grow up and make decisions that will not always please us. However, we can know that regardless of the obstacles each one faces, the Word of God will light his pathway. He will hear a voice saying, "This is the way. Walk in it." When he goes out, he will not be lost.

You are the primary representatives of God in the life of your child. God made a covenant with Abraham and declared, "I will continue this everlasting covenant between us, generation after generation. It will continue between me and your offspring forever" (Gen. 17:7, NLT). Through the work of Christ Jesus, God has blessed the Gentiles with the same blessing He promised to Abraham (Gal. 3:14). You have the ability to pass these blessings on to your child.

After Adam and Eve sinned, God said to the serpent, "From now on, you and the woman will be enemies, and your offspring and her offspring will be enemies. He will crush your head, and you will strike his heel" (Gen. 3:15, NLT). Since that time Satan has determined to destroy the woman and her seed. BUT GOD!

This book is intended to inspire parents and caregivers to bless aloud their children. Blessing and praying scriptural prayers will give an all-encompassing and more in-depth view of God's will for the life of each child. The Holy Spirit uses spiritual words, and He gives you the wisdom to point the child in the right direction.

God chose your child before the foundation of the world to be made whole and holy by His love. His intent is that you will take him/her by the hand and lead him/her in the way of the Master.

We have the opportunity to train and develop the future generation in the ways and purposes of God, and it begins with prayer and blessing. Years ago I knew a Sunday school teacher who loved to teach the preschool and early elementary school children. She said that their hearts were tender and their minds eager to learn, and they believed the words she spoke to them. Your child begins learning the moment he enters the world.

Together we can teach the next generation His ways of doing and being right. We don't want our children to become so well-adjusted to our culture that they fit into it without even thinking.

It is up to you to choose right words to speak over your child. Out of the abundance of the heart the mouth speaks. Be God-minded, learn His ways and His thoughts and hide His Word in your heart. Live truly, speak truly and deal truly in all the affairs of life. "A person's words can be life-giving water; words of true wisdom are as refreshing as a bubbling brook" (Prov. 18:4, NLT).

The importance of a mother's voice became apparent at the birth of our last grandchild. As the pediatrician and nurse were cleaning him up, they discovered that they needed to take him to the nursery due to excessive fluid in his respiratory system.

Our daughter asked if she could see him before they took him away. They swaddled him in blankets while he proved to one and all that he could make himself heard. The doctor walked over to the bed with the crying child and placed him in his mother's arms. It was astounding as we watched with tears in our eyes. At the sound of his mother's voice, the child immediately hushed and listened while his mother spoke comforting words to him.

The blessings recorded in this book are intended for you as parents to speak and pray before the heavenly Father in the hearing of your child; they can be repeated as he matures. Give him Jesus—give him Life!

Even though he may not intellectually comprehend the true meaning, his memory is recording all that he hears. Your child is spirit, soul and body, and he is internalizing the words he hears. The Holy Spirit will give him understanding as he develops. The entrance of God's Word gives light.

I encourage you to pray in the hearing of your child every day. Blessing your child, speaking words that are spirit and life, will elevate your thinking from the temporal to the eternal. God will give you the wisdom to train up your child in the way that he should go.

Your child is created in the image of God. He is created for God's purpose, and he has an eternal destiny. Parents are the custodians of these children who in reality belong to God and are for His pleasure.

As parents we do not know the obstacles and challenges that our children will face. I recently heard the testimony of a teenager who had a stroke when he was ten years old. His obstacles have been monumental and difficult, but not impossible.

He had to learn to talk and to walk. He now uses his left hand to draw, and his paintings are winning awards and selling. He plans to attend college even though it will be more difficult and challenging. Prepare your child for his future so that his faith will not fail him when he has to move mountains.

God is watching over His Word to perform it. The Word of God that you speak will not return void, without accomplishing His purpose. God will not fail one word of His promise. You will be encouraged and built up spiritually as you read and meditate on the blessings contained in the following pages. Be blessed!

JANUARY

Welcome to the Family

January

WELCOME TO GOD'S FAMILY

What a wonderful day it is to welcome a new child into the family! The psalmist wrote, "Sons are a heritage from the Lord, children a reward from him. Like arrows in the hands of a warrior are sons born in one's youth. Blessed is the man whose quiver is full of them. They will not be put to shame when they contend with their enemies in the gate" (Ps. 127:3–5, NIV).

Yes, this is a great day; you have much to be thankful for! All things in your young child's life are brand-new. A great honor has been bestowed upon you because God has placed in your care this young child that He created in His own image. The days ahead will be full of the joys of that first smile, first word, first tooth and first step. All of these are part of your child's journey toward receiving Jesus Christ as his personal Lord and Savior and fulfilling the destiny for which God created him.

Of course, the great honor of being a parent also comes with great responsibility. As your child begins his journey in the life that lies before him, his needs for food, shelter, love, protection and guidance must be met if he is to be physically and emotionally healthy. Because this helpless child has been placed in your care, God has now given you the privilege and responsibility of providing for those needs. However, it is important to remember that your child's needs do not stop there. His welfare is also dependent upon his spiritual needs being met. "We will tell the next generation the praiseworthy deeds of the Lord, his power, and the wonders he has done" (Ps. 78:4, NIV).

Fortunately, only one day comes at a time, and you are not alone. You have a Comforter, a Helper, who will guide you into all truth. In John 15:26 Jesus speaks of the Holy Spirit when He says, "But when the Comforter is come, whom I will send unto you from the Father, even the Spirit of truth, which proceedeth from the Father, he shall testify of me" (KJV).

The happiest home is one that is a house of prayer, a place where your days together begin and end with prayer, praises to God and spoken words of blessing. In fact, your very life can be a prayer to God; each moment can be an expression of thanksgiving and praise to Him. "Then we your people, the sheep of your pasture, will praise you forever; from generation to generation we will recount your praise" (Ps. 79:13, NIV).

Your family will be knit together in faith, joy and love when you set aside a time at the beginning and end of each day to pray, praise and thank God and to speak words of life and blessing over your child. Because the blessings and prayers in this book are taken from the Word of God, you will be anchored together in Truth.

We can begin to see the importance of this by looking at Jesus' expression of His own love for the little children. In Isaiah 40:11 we see a beautiful picture of Jesus and His little lambs: "He shall gather the lambs with his arm, and carry them in his bosom" (KJV). Then in Mark 10:16 we see this same picture: "And he took the children in his arms, put his hands on them and blessed them" (NIV). Because He has entrusted you as the parent of His little lamb, you have been given the wonderful opportunity to stand in the Lord's stead over your child. You are Jesus' arms when you take your precious child in your arms; you are Jesus' hands when you lay your hands on him; you are

Jesus' mouth when you speak words of life and truth over him.

Not only will your words and prayers release blessings to your child, but these words will also be a lamp unto your own feet. They will remind you of the wonderful plans God has for your child and for your family. The blessings, prayers and Scripture readings will give you vision and clarity, and they will deepen your understanding of your purpose as a parent. They will give you a standard by which to live. They will bring to remembrance the splendors and wonders of God, thereby igniting joy, thanksgiving and faith.

Day 1

MORNING

______, we bless you in the name of Jesus, and we thank our heavenly Father for building our family. May you be God's instrument for noble purposes, made holy, useful to the Master and prepared to do any good work He has prepared for you to do.

EVENING

I thank Father God for you, my precious child. You were created for God's good pleasure. Long before God laid down earth's foundations, He had you in mind. He settled on you as the focus of His love.

Scripture Reading
Psalm 128:3–4
2 Timothy 2:21
Genesis 1:26
Ephesians 1:4, The Message

Day 2

MORNING

Little one, I bless you and welcome you into our family in the name of Jesus. I welcome Jesus' presence here. Father God created you for His pleasure according to His will.

EVENING

I bow before God at the close of the day, and I embrace you, ______, as a heritage from God. You are my reward—a perfect gift sent to me from above. May you fulfill God's divine destiny and bring glory to Him.

Scripture Reading
Mark 9:37
Revelation 4:11, NKJV
Psalm 127:3
James 1:17

Day 3

MORNING

I bless you, my child, on this day that God has made. God made you a little lower than the heavenly beings and crowned you with glory and honor. I am confident that God will send you in the right direction.

EVENING

______, God watched you from conception to birth. All the stages of your life are spread out before the Lord. He prepared the days of your life before you even lived one day. ______, I bless you and ask the Father to lead you forth in peace.

Scripture Reading

Psalm 8:5
Psalm 23:3, THE MESSAGE
Psalm 139:16, THE MESSAGE
Isaiah 55:12, NIV

Day 4

MORNING

May you grow in the nurture and admonition of the Lord, and may you be an instrument of God's peace, filled with compassion for the less fortunate. I bring you to the Lord Jesus, and Him to you.

EVENING

I embrace you with God's love that is shed abroad in our hearts by the Holy Spirit. May God give you the grace to love Him because He first loved you. I embrace you as God embraces us, and I embrace Him who sent you.

Scripture Reading
Matthew 19:14, The Message
Mark 9:37, The Message

Day 5

MORNING

May our Father God write mercy and truth upon the tablets of your heart. May you be blessed by the Father to find favor and good understanding with God and with man.

EVENING

I have asked our Father God to contend with those who would contend with us, and to give you safety and ease day by day.

Scripture Reading
Proverbs 3:3–4
Isaiah 49:26, AMP

Day 6

MORNING

I bless you to be a disciple of Christ, taught of the Lord and obedient to God's will. Great shall be your peace and undisturbed composure. May you mature and grow in the grace and knowledge of our Lord and Savior Jesus Christ. I dedicate you to the Father.

EVENING

Here at the close of another day, I commit you into God's hands, and I am positively persuaded that God is able to guard and keep that which I have committed to Him. I thank God for giving sweet sleep to you.

Scripture Reading
Isaiah 54:13, AMP
2 Peter 3:18
2 Timothy 1:12

Day 7

MORNING

I believe God's promises. He said, "My Holy Spirit shall not leave your children; they shall want the good and hate the wrong—they and their children and their children's children forever." I thank God for performing His Word in your life.

EVENING

I thank God for giving His angels charge over you to accompany, defend and preserve you in all your ways. God is your refuge and fortress. He is the glory and the lifter of your head.

Scripture Reading
Isaiah 59:21
Jeremiah 1:12
Psalm 91:2, 11
Psalm 3:3

Day 8

MORNING

God dearly loves you, and you feel this warm love everywhere within you. His eye is on you because I respect Him; I hope in His unfailing love.

EVENING

I pray for good fortune in everything you do and for your good health, so that your everyday affairs will prosper as well as your soul! Nothing will make me happier than knowing that you will continue diligently in the way of Truth!

Scripture Reading

Romans 5:5, TLB
Psalm 33:18 NIV, THE MESSAGE
3 John 2, 4, THE MESSAGE

Day 9

MORNING

I commit to teach you God's ways, to help you listen and hear instruction, to help you pay attention and gain understanding. You will lay hold of God's words with all of your heart, and you will keep God's Word.

EVENING

God has provided for everything you could possibly need, and He has abounded toward you with all prudence and wisdom. You will learn to be wise. You will develop good judgment and common sense! You will love and cling to Wisdom—she will protect and guard you in the name of Jesus.

Scripture Reading
Proverbs 4:1–2, 4, NIV
Ephesians 1:8, KJV, THE MESSAGE
Proverbs 4:5–6

Day 10

MORNING

In Jesus' name, I bless you and pray that you will find grace in God's eyes. His grace is sufficient for any situation, and He will give you courage to overcome every obstacle. I ask God to create in you the desire to be ever learning, ever growing and ever achieving as you grow in the grace and the knowledge of our Lord Jesus Christ.

EVENING

Jesus has been made unto you wisdom, righteousness and sanctification. May you have right standing with our Father who is in heaven. I have covenant with our heavenly Father in the name of Jesus, and I ask that you will be righteous before Him in your generation.

Scripture Reading
Genesis 6:8
2 Corinthians 12:9
2 Peter 3:18
Isaiah 59:21
Genesis 7:1
1 Corinthians 1:30
Matthew 6:9

Day 11

MORNING

God has given you a spirit of power, love and self-discipline. I pray that you will not be afraid. He is your shield, your exceedingly great reward.

EVENING

May God Almighty bless you, make you fruitful and multiply you according to His will. I dedicate you to Christ. You are Abraham's offspring and spiritual heir according to promise.

Scripture Reading
2 Timothy 1:7
Genesis 15:1
Genesis 28:3–4, AMP
Galatians 3:29

Day 12

MORNING

I pray that the Father will watch over you when I am absent and we are hidden from one another. I ask Him to cover you with His feathers. Under His wings you shall take refuge. I thank God that you are never alone.

EVENING

God will be with you in all that you do, and He will make you prosper. You will be like a tree planted by the rivers of water that brings forth fruit in its season. Your leaf shall not wither, and whatever you do shall prosper.

Scripture Reading
Genesis 31:49, AMP
Psalm 91:4–5
Genesis 39:23, AMP
Psalm 1

Day 13

MORNING

May you be blessed with the blessings from heaven above. How I praise God, the Father of our Lord Jesus Christ, who has blessed you with every blessing in heaven because you are prepared for God (pure and clean).

EVENING

May Jehovah reveal Himself to you as the Almighty, who is all powerful and ever present. He is the same yesterday, today and forever. I pray that you will know that there is no one like Him.

Scripture Reading

Genesis 49:25, NKJV
Ephesians 1:3
1 Corinthians 14, AMP
Exodus 3:14–15
Hebrews 13:8
Exodus 8:10

MORNING

This morning I praise the Lord. When He formed you, He made your mouth to praise Him. I ask the Lord to help me to teach you to speak of excellent things. May the opening of your lips be for right things, and may you always say what is good and helpful to others.

EVENING

At the close of another day, I worship God. May you, my child, live within the shadow of the Almighty, sheltered by the God who is above all gods. None is like unto Him, glorious in holiness, awesome in splendor, doing wonders.

Scripture Reading
Exodus 4:11–12, NKJV
Proverbs 8:6, KJV
Ephesians 4:29, TLB
Exodus 15:11, AMP
Psalm 91:1, TLB

Day 15

MORNING

May God bless you with His mercy and steadfast love. His mercy and steadfast love shall extend to a thousand generations after you because He gave you a heart to love Him and keep His commandments.

EVENING

I ask the Father to send an angel before you to keep and guard you on the way and to lead you to the destiny He has prepared for you. You are His workmanship, created in Christ Jesus to do good works, which He prepared in advance for you to do.

Scripture Reading
Exodus 20:6, AMP
Exodus 23:20, AMP
Ephesians 2:10, NIV

Day 16

MORNING

May the Lord fill you with the Spirit of God, wisdom, ability, understanding, intelligence, knowledge and all kinds of craftsmanship for His glory. I ask the Lord to direct your education so that you may be strong, healthy, well-read in many fields, well-informed, alert and sensible, and have poise before your teachers and peers.

EVENING

______, I bless you and pray that you may be privileged to find favor in the sight of God. I ask the Father to reveal to you His ways that you may know Him. I ask Him to grant His grace and peace to you many times over as you deepen in your relationship with Him.

Scripture Reading
Exodus 31:3, AMP
Daniel 1:4, TLB
Exodus 33:13–14, AMP
2 Peter 1:2

Day 17

MORNING

I thank the Lord for the beginning of another day. He will teach you to regard Him as holy so that your life may glorify Him before all people. Great will be your peace as the Lord teaches you His ways.

EVENING

May the Father create a desire in you to keep the way of the Lord by doing what is right and just, so He can bring about what He has promised. I pray that you will live according to God's ways, in the name of Jesus.

Scripture Reading
Isaiah 54:13, NIV
Leviticus 10:3, NKJV
Genesis 18:19, NIV
Leviticus 18:5

Day 18

MORNING

May you walk in the merciful Father's ways so that you will live safely and peacefully in a fruitful land. I ask Him to grant you the grace to walk in all the ways that He has commanded you, so that you may live, prosper and prolong your days on earth.

EVENING

I pray that the Lord will look favorably on you, causing you to be fruitful and confirming His covenant. Walk with Him, for He is your God. Grow in stature and in favor with the Lord and with men.

Scripture Reading
Leviticus 25:18–19, NKJV
Deuteronomy 5:33
Leviticus 26:9, 12, NKJV
1 Samuel 2:26

Day 19

MORNING

I ask the Lord to bless you and keep you, to show you His kindness and to have mercy on you. I thank Him for watching over you and giving you peace.

EVENING

I ask the Lord God to give you the ability to see obstacles and challenges through eyes of faith as Caleb did. By His power, He has made you more than able to overcome.[1]

Scripture Reading
Numbers 6:24–26, NCV
Numbers 13:30

Day 20

MORNING

I pray to the Lord our God that you will not be terrified or afraid. He goes before you. He has not given you a spirit of fear, but of power, love and a sound mind.

EVENING

I pray to the Lord that you will not turn aside to the right hand or to the left. I ask Him to give you a heart to walk in all His ways that He has commanded you so that you may live, that it may be well with you and that He will prolong your days on earth.

Scripture Reading
Deuteronomy 1:29
2 Timothy 1:7
Deuteronomy 5:32–33, NKJV

Day 21

MORNING

God is faithful, and He has called you, my child, into the fellowship of His Son, Jesus Christ our Lord. I bless you that you may know that He keeps covenant and mercy for a thousand generations with those who love Him and obey His commands.

EVENING

I ask the Father to give you a wise mind and spirit that is attuned to His will so that you may acquire a thorough understanding of the ways in which He works. May you choose to do what is true and fair and find all the good trails!

Scripture Reading
1 Corinthians 1:9, NKJV
Deuteronomy 7:9 NKJV, TLB
Colossians 1:9, THE MESSAGE
Proverbs 2:9, THE MESSAGE

Day 22

MORNING

I ask the Lord to give you insight to do what He tells you. May your whole life be one long, obedient response. I pray that you will store His words in your heart and soul, binding them as a sign on your hands and keeping them ever before your eyes.

EVENING

May the Lord help you to live generously and to open your eyes to see the poor around you so that you will give freely and willingly to meet the needs of others.

Scripture Reading
Psalm 119:34, The Message
Deuteronomy 11:18, NKJV
Matthew 5:42, The Message
Deuteronomy 15:8, NKJV

Day 23

MORNING

I thank God for the tranquillity we have this morning. Old things have passed away, and behold, all things have become new. I loose you from the influence of wrong words spoken about you or to you. I pray that God will turn any curse into a blessing.

EVENING

May the Lord God give you an obedient heart so you will carefully follow all His commands. As you obey the Lord, all of His blessings will come upon you, and you will eat the best from the land.

Scripture Reading
2 Corinthians 5:17–18
Deuteronomy 23:5, NKJV
Deuteronomy 28:1–2, NIV
Isaiah 1:19, NIV

MORNING

I pray for the Lord to bless your skills and be pleased with the work of your hands. I thank God for creating a desire in you to work, to do something useful with your own hands so you may have something to share with those in need.

EVENING

May the Father create a kind heart and desire in you to bless others. As you bless others, you will be abundantly blessed. As you help others, you will be abundantly helped. As you are kind and merciful, you will be shown abundant mercy.

Scripture Reading
Deuteronomy 33:11, NIV
Ephesians 4:28, NIV
Proverbs 11:25, The Message
Matthew 5:7, TLB

Day 25

MORNING

I pray that you will be strong and very courageous, that you will have success wherever you go as you act according to all of the Word of God. May the words of your mouth and the meditation of your heart be pleasing in the Lord's sight. He is your Rock and your Redeemer.

EVENING

May you know that not one thing has failed of all the good things which have been spoken concerning you.

Scripture Reading

Joshua 1:7, NKJV
Psalm 19:14, NIV
Joshua 23:14
Joshua 21:45

Day 26

MORNING

I pray that you will revere and fear the Lord, serve Him and hearken to His voice. I ask Him to create in you an obedient heart so you will not rebel against His commandments. As you follow the Lord your God, it will be good!

EVENING

May the Lord teach you to hear His voice and to be quick to obey Him, for obedience is better than sacrifice.[2]

Scripture Reading
1 Samuel 12:14, AMP
1 Samuel 15:22
Psalm 119:60, The Message

Day 27

MORNING

I ask the Lord to show kindness and faithfulness to you. May you strengthen your hands and be valiant. I pray that out of His glorious riches He will strengthen you through His Spirit with power in your inner being.

EVENING

May the Lord God reveal His greatness to you. There is none like Him, nor is there any God besides Him.[3] His way is holy! No god is great like God!

Scripture Reading
2 Samuel 2:6–7, AMP
Ephesians 3:16, NIV
2 Samuel 7:22
Psalm 77:13

Day 28

MORNING

I pray that you will walk in His ways so that you may prosper in all you do and in every place you go. You shall flourish like a palm tree and grow tall as the cedars of Lebanon. You are inside the Christian covenant, prepared for God, pure and clean.

EVENING

May God give you, ______, an understanding heart like Solomon's to discern between good and evil. As you mature and practice doing what is right, you will learn right from wrong.

Scripture Reading

1 Kings 2:3, NKJV
Psalm 92:12, NIV
1 Corinthians 7:14, AMP
1 Kings 3:9, NKJV
Hebrews 5:14, TLB

Day 29

MORNING

I pray that God will give you rest and peace in all areas of your life and that He will keep evil far from you.[4] Evil cannot come close to you; it cannot get through the door because God has ordered His angels to guard you wherever you go.

EVENING

______, you will not be afraid. God is your shield and your abundant compensation. Your reward shall be exceedingly great. God will help you to be on your guard, to stand firm in the faith and to become a man (or woman) of courage. ______, I bless you with strength.

Scripture Reading

1 Kings 5:4
Psalm 91:10–11, The Message
Genesis 15:1, AMP
1 Corinthians 16:13, NIV

Day 30

MORNING

God did not give you a spirit of fear. Because those who are with you are more than those who are against you, you will not be afraid. I thank God for giving angels special charge over you to accompany, defend and preserve you in all your ways of obedience and service to Him.

EVENING

I pray that in your youth you will do what is right in God's eyes, not turning aside to the right nor to the left as you follow only Him. May your sons, in their prime of lives, be as sturdy oak trees, and may your daughters be as shapely as bright fields of wildflowers.

Scripture Reading
2 Timothy 1:7
2 Kings 6:16
Psalm 91:11–12, AMP
2 Kings 22:2
Psalm 144:12, The Message

Day 31

MORNING

May the Lord give you an understanding of the times. He chose you before the foundation of the world for such a time as this. He planned the paths on which you should walk.

EVENING

With praise and thanksgiving, you will sing to the Lord, saying, "You are good; Your love endures forever." You will praise God's name in song and glorify Him with thanksgiving.

Scripture Reading

1 Chronicles 12:32
Ephesians 1:4; 2:10, AMP
Esther 4:14, TLB
Ezra 3:11, TLB
Psalm 69:30, NIV

FEBRUARY

God's Protection

PARENTAL BLESSINGS

We do not have to look far to find accounts of parents blessing their own children. Examples of this include Noah blessing two of his sons (Gen. 9:26–27), Isaac blessing his sons (Gen. 27:27–29, 39–40, 28:3–4), and the words of blessing that Jacob spoke over his sons (Gen. 49:1–28). In each case, these patriarchs of the faith spoke words of prophecy that the Lord had revealed would happen to their children. If we study the Scriptures, we find that in each case the words these men spoke over their sons did indeed come to pass.

If we look at Hebrews 11:20–21, we see that speaking a blessing over our children is an act of faith. It was by faith that Isaac blessed his own sons: "By faith Isaac blessed Jacob and Esau in regard to their future" (v. 20, NIV). It was also by faith that Jacob blessed Joseph's sons: "By faith Jacob, when he was dying, blessed each of Joseph's sons, and worshiped as he leaned on the top of his staff" (v. 21, NIV). Both of these men spoke the words the Lord laid upon their hearts in advance of the events occurring. In Hebrews 11:39 we are told that these men were commended for their faith.

In turn, we can also bind our faith to the Word of God when we speak blessings over our own children and grandchildren. We have been given the written Word of God, and we can stand steadfast in faith that what is written in the Scriptures will indeed come to pass in the lives of our children. When we speak blessings that are based upon the Word of God, we are agreeing with the

Word of God. Just as the patriarchs spoke out in faith that what the Lord had revealed to their hearts would come to pass, we can speak the Word of the Lord that has been revealed in the Scriptures and by His Spirit.

Examples of parental blessings are recorded in the New Testament as well as in the Old Testament. An example of a parental blessing is seen in Zechariah's song of prophecy after the birth of his son John (the Baptist). After Zechariah had written on a tablet, "His name is John," he was able to speak again, and he began to praise God. The people were filled with awe about the events that surrounded the birth of this child, including how Zechariah had been stricken dumb while he was in the temple. Because the people were wondering about these events, they began asking, "'What then is this child going to be?' For the Lord's hand was with him" (Luke 1:66, NIV). John's father Zechariah was then filled with the Holy Spirit and prophesied. First, he praised the Lord and spoke of His wonderful deeds, and then he prophesied about his own son. "And you, my child, will be called a prophet of the Most High; for you will go on before the Lord to prepare the way for him, to give his people the knowledge of salvation through the forgiveness of sins, because of the tender mercy of our God" (vv. 76–78, NIV). These words that Zechariah spoke (or sung) over his child did indeed come to pass. "And the child grew and became strong in spirit; and he lived in the desert until he appeared publicly to Israel" (v. 80, NIV).

As you speak the Word of the Lord over your own child, praise Him and thank Him for His mighty deeds and for what He is going to do in the life of your child and in your family as a whole. The Word of God is sure and true. You can depend upon it. "Above all, you must understand that no prophecy of Scripture came about by the prophet's own interpretation. For prophecy never had its origin in the will of man, but men spoke from God as they were carried along by the Holy Spirit" (2 Pet. 1:20–21, NIV).

As you speak blessings over your child, you can be confident that the Word of the Lord will indeed come to pass, and that His Word will not come back void to Him.

Day 1

MORNING

I pray that you will walk straight, act right and tell the truth. I thank the Lord that you will obtain grace and favor in His sight. He is a sun and shield. He bestows favor and honor, and He will not withhold any good thing from you. ______, you will walk uprightly before the Lord.

EVENING

May Father God give you the desire and courage to rise to each and every challenge before you, for He may have placed you in these situations for such a time as this.[5] His grace is sufficient for you, dear child. His power is made perfect in weakness.

Scripture Reading
Psalm 15:2, The Message
Esther 2:17
Psalm 84:11, KJV
Esther 4:14
2 Corinthians 12:9, NIV

Day 2

MORNING

I ask God to create a hunger for His Word in your heart. His Word will thrill you, and you will be nourished by Scripture day and night. You are a tree replanted in Eden, bearing fresh fruit every month, never dropping a leaf, always in blossom.

EVENING

I thank God for shielding you on all sides, for grounding your feet and for lifting your head high. The Lord God is your strength and your shield. Your heart will trust in the Lord, and He will help you in every situation.

Scripture Reading
Psalm 1:2–3, The Message
Psalm 3:3
Psalm 28:7

MORNING

God is with you. He has promised to protect you wherever you go and to bring you back safely. He will be with you constantly until He has finished giving you all He has promised.

EVENING

May the Lord bless and protect you; may His face radiate with joy because of you. May He be gracious to you, show you His favor and give you His peace.

Scripture Reading
Genesis 28:15, TLB
Numbers 6:24

MORNING

May the Lord bless you and protect you with His shield of love as though He is protecting the pupil of His own eye, hiding you in the shadow of His wings as He hovers over you.

EVENING

May the Lord bless you with the revelation of Himself, thereby giving you clear signposts that point out the right road on which you are to walk. May integrity and uprightness protect you, because our hope is in God.

Scripture Reading
Psalm 5:12, TLB
Psalm 17:8
Psalm 19:7, THE MESSAGE
Psalm 25:21, NIV

MORNING

God's faithfulness, mercy and loving-kindness shall be with you, and in His name shall your strength be exalted. Great power and prosperity shall be conferred upon you as you grow in the grace of spiritual strength, knowledge and understanding of our Lord and Savior Jesus Christ.

EVENING

The Lord has blessed you with divine protection. Just as the mountains surround and protect Jerusalem, so He surrounds and protects you. You will embrace Wisdom, and she will keep you, defend you and protect you. I thank God for creating a love for Wisdom in you that will guard you.

Scripture Reading
Psalm 89:24, AMP
2 Peter 3:18
Psalm 125:2, TLB
Proverbs 4:6, AMP

MORNING

I acknowledge God at the beginning of another day. I ask Him to help you maintain sound and godly wisdom and discretion throughout your days, for they will be success to you, keeping you safe from defeat and disaster and from stumbling off the godly trail.

EVENING

I thank the Lord for the good things that happened today. I am grateful for the angel of the Lord who is encamped round about our home. He is most careful with us.

Scripture Reading

Proverbs 3:21–22, AMP
Proverbs 3:23, TLB
Psalm 34:7
1 Peter 5:7, THE MESSAGE

Day 7

MORNING

The Lord shall be strong in you. He will not let your hands be weak and slack, for your work shall be rewarded. Many shall stand amazed at your success because He is your mighty protector.

EVENING

Your heavenly Father pays attention to us, and you can relax. You can take it easy—you are in good hands. You will lie down in peace and sleep here in this room; the Lord will keep you safe.

Scripture Reading
2 Chronicles 15:7, AMP
Psalm 71:7, TLB
Proverbs 1:33
Psalm 4:8

MORNING

I ask the Lord to give you understanding and a heart to be just and fair in everything you do. He has called you to be a leader in your generation. Like the horizons for breadth and the ocean for depth, the understanding of a good leader is broad and deep.

EVENING

May the Lord overlook youthful sins and look at you through eyes of mercy and forgiveness, through eyes of everlasting love and kindness. Let His loving-kindness and truth preserve you continually.

Scripture Reading
Proverbs 1:3, TLB
Proverbs 25:3, The Message
Psalm 25:7
Psalm 40:11

Day 9

MORNING

May the Holy Spirit lead you to the Most High God. I proclaim that God is your place of safety and protection. He is our God, and I trust Him.

EVENING

I thank God for saving you from hidden traps and from deadly diseases. He will cover you with His feathers, and under His wings you can hide. His truth will be your shield and protection.

Scripture Reading
Psalm 91:1–2, NCV

Day 10

MORNING

When troubles rise like a flood, they will not reach you. God is your hiding place. He protects you from troubles and fills you with songs of salvation.

EVENING

God is your protection and strength. Because He always helps in times of trouble, you will not be afraid even if the earth shakes, the mountains fall into the sea or the oceans roar and foam.

Scripture Reading
Psalm 32:6–7, NCV
Psalm 46:1–2, NCV

Day 11

MORNING

My child, I pray for you to understand that the ways of God are without fault; the Lord's words are pure. He is a shield to all that trust Him. God is your protection, and He makes your way free from fault.

EVENING

______, I bless you with God's protection. I ask the Lord to make you like a deer that does not stumble, to help you stand on the steep mountains. I thank God for protecting you with His saving shield and that He has stooped to make you great. May God give you the grace to live as He wants you to.

Scripture Reading
2 Samuel 22:31–32, NCV
2 Samuel 22:34–35

Day 12

MORNING

I pray that you will serve God all the days of your life. God is strong, and He will help you walk in His ways. May He bring you before His glory without any wrong in you and give you great joy. He is the only God, the One who saves you.

EVENING

My child, I pray that you will always remember that your help comes from the Lord, who made heaven and earth. He will not let you be defeated; He never sleeps. The Lord guards you. He is the shade that protects you from all dangers; He will guard your life as you come and go, both now and forever.

Scripture Reading
Jude 24, NCV
Psalm 121, NCV

Day 13

MORNING

I bless you with the experiential knowledge of unconditional love. I pray for the Father to draw you to Himself. You will call upon His name and be saved.

EVENING

I ask the all-powerful Lord to bless you with knowledge and understanding that you may honor Him. Goodness will shine on you like the sun, with healing in its rays. You will jump around, like a well-fed calf.

Scripture Reading
Joel 2:32
Malachi 4:2–3

Day 14

MORNING

My child, God looked over all that He had made and saw that it was excellent in every way. I ask the Lord to help you to develop your abilities and assume your responsibilities in a way that reflects His nature in all of creation.[6]

EVENING

I bind your spirit, soul and body, ______, to God's mercy and grace. I pray that you will see the Son and believe in Him. You will have eternal life, and He will raise you on the last day. This is what He wants for you, and I praise Him for His salvation.

Scripture Reading
Genesis 1:26, 27–31
John 6:40

Day 15

MORNING

May Jesus anoint your ears to hear what He says and to believe in the Father who sent Him, so that you shall have eternal life.

EVENING

I proclaim that you, ______, shall be one who listens to the voice of our God. You will know Him, and you will follow Him. He will give you eternal life, and you shall never perish. No one can snatch you out of the Father's hand.

Scripture Reading
John 5:21

Day 16

MORNING

I thank Father God for Jesus, who came as light into the world, so that you will believe and not live in darkness. You will call on the name of the Lord and be saved.

EVENING

I believe it is through the grace of our Lord Jesus that you, ______, will be saved. For it is by grace that we are saved through faith. It is the gift of God, not by works, so that no one can boast.

Scripture Reading

John 12:44–46, NCV
Acts 2:21
Acts 15:11
Ephesians 2:8–9

Day 17

MORNING

I thank God for providing a Friend, a Counselor, for you so that you will always have Someone with you. This Friend is the Spirit of Truth. You shall know Him, and He will stay with you and even be in you!

EVENING

May the Lord create a desire in you to ask Him for one thing: to live with Him in His house your whole life long. There you will contemplate His beauty and study at His feet. That is the only quiet, secure place in a noisy world, the perfect getaway, far from the buzz of traffic.

Scripture Reading
John 14:16–17, THE MESSAGE
Psalm 27:4–7, THE MESSAGE

Day 18

MORNING

I thank God for holding your head and shoulders above all those who would try to pull you down. You are headed for His place to offer anthems that will raise the roof! Already you are singing God's songs; you are making music to the Lord.

EVENING

May you have a heart and mind to trust God all the time. You will tell Him all of your problems because He is your protection.

Scripture Reading
Psalm 27:6
Psalm 62:8, NCV

Day 19

MORNING

Here I am before the Lord with you, my little one, eyes open, drinking in His strength and glory. In His generous love you are really living at last! Your lips brim praises like fountains. You will bless Him every time you take a breath; your arms wave like banners of praise to God.

EVENING

God is always with you, and He will hold your hand. I ask Him to guide you with His advice, and later He will receive you in honor.

Scripture Reading
Psalm 63:3–4, The Message
Psalm 73:23–24

Day 20

MORNING

I pray for and bless you, ______, May God always remain close to you. He is your protection. You will tell your generation about all that God has done.

EVENING

May God bless you with clean hands and a pure heart. You will not worship idols. You will receive a blessing from the Lord. The Lord God, who saves you, will declare you right. You will follow God.

Scripture Reading
Psalm 73:28
Psalm 24:4–6, NIV

Day 21

MORNING

I ask the Lord to bless you with His love. I pray that you will glory in His holy name. May the Lord give you a heart to seek Him and rejoice. May you look to Him and His strength. May you seek His face always.

EVENING

May God give you, ______, a heart to worship Him, and He will protect you. May He give you the grace to trust Him, and He will save you. I dedicate you to God, and He will give you happiness.

Scripture Reading
Psalm 105:3–4, NIV
Psalm 86:1–4, NCV

MORNING

I bless you, and I pray that as you grow older, you will listen to God. He has ordered peace for you, and you will worship Him. May God keep you from foolishness and save you, for you shall respect the Lord.

EVENING

Little one, I pray for you to receive love and truth, for they belong to God's people. Goodness and mercy shall follow you all the days of your life.

Scripture Reading
Psalm 85:8–9
Psalm 85:10
Psalm 23:6

Day 23

MORNING

I bless you and pray that as you grow older, you will desire to seek first the kingdom of God and His righteousness. All things pertaining to life and godliness will be added unto you.

EVENING

The Father blessed you by choosing you before the foundation of the world. I believe that as you grow up, you will love the Lord your God with all your heart, with all your soul and with all your strength.

Scripture Reading
Matthew 6:33
Ephesians 1:4
Deuteronomy 6:5

Day 24

MORNING

God's Word is a lamp to your feet and a light for your path. His plans will be your plans, and God will enable you to live them.

EVENING

I bless you, my little one, this evening. May God always protect you with salvation-armor, hold you up with a firm hand and caress you with His gentle ways. I thank God for hearing us when we pray.

Scripture Reading
Psalm 119:105
Proverbs 16, THE MESSAGE
Psalm 18:35, THE MESSAGE

Day 25

MORNING

I bow before the Father this morning. I declare that every bone in your body is laughing and singing the words, "God, there's no one like You." I ask the Lord to pick you up and put you on your feet when you are feeling down and to protect you from your enemies.

EVENING

I trust in the Lord. May His huge, outstretched arms protect you. Under them, you are perfectly safe; His arms fend off all harm. I thank God for loving you, my child.

Scripture Reading
Psalm 35:10, The Message
Psalm 91:4, The Message

Day 26

MORNING

I bless you, little one. The Lord watches over you—the Lord is your shade at His right hand. God is your Guardian, right at your side to protect you. May you always know truth.

EVENING

I thank God for keeping you safe. I ask God to keep you out of the clutches of the wicked and protect you from vicious people. God, our Lord, is a strong Savior.

Scripture Reading
Psalm 121:5, NIV, THE MESSAGE
Psalm 140:1, 4, 7, NIV, THE MESSAGE

Day 27

MORNING

Little one, I bless you. Even while you are here in my protection, I pray that God will go before you and rescue you from the grip of unwholesome men and women so that you can live life God's way.

EVENING

May the Father give you, my little one, the compassion of Jesus that you may rescue the perishing, without hesitating to step in and help. May God give you a desire to bless the poor and those less fortunate than you.

Scripture Reading
Psalm 119:134, The Message
Proverbs 24:11, The Message

Day 28

MORNING

I thank God for welcoming you with open arms when you run to Him for cover. May He spread His protection over you that He may rejoice in you because you love His name.

EVENING

I thank God for blessing you, keeping watch over you and keeping you out of trouble. I am assured that He will be there when you run to Him.

Scripture Reading
Psalm 5:11, NIV, THE MESSAGE
Psalm 25:20, THE MESSAGE

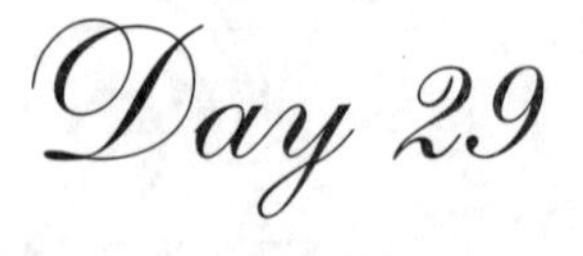

Day 29

MORNING

Bless you, my child. May you be enthroned in God's presence forever. I ask God, our Father, to appoint His love and faithfulness to protect you.

EVENING

I ask the Lord to guard your life, for I am devoted to Him. He is our God. I ask Him to save you, my beloved child, for I trust in Him. He has ordered the angels to guard you wherever you go.

Scripture Reading
Psalm 61:7, NIV
Psalm 86:2

MARCH

Created for His Pleasure

March

YOUR CHILD'S DESTINY

As a child of God, your young child has a glorious calling to fellowship with Christ (1 Cor. 1:9), to holiness (1 Thess. 4:7), to a prize (Phil. 3:14), to liberty (Gal. 5:13), to peace (1 Cor. 7:15), to glory and virtue (2 Pet. 1:3), to the eternal glory of Christ (2 Thess. 2:14) and to eternal life (1 Tim. 6:12). Certainly this is not a complete list, but it is clear that because of Jesus Christ your child is very special and has an eternal destiny. She is a beauty and wonder to behold in the eyes of God. His love for her is so great that God the Father gave His only begotten Son for her, so that she would spend eternity with Him. He is her Father God. He is her eternal heavenly Father. "As a father has compassion on his children, so the Lord has compassion on those who fear him; for he knows how we are formed, he remembers that we are dust" (Ps. 103:13–14, NIV).

Jesus Christ died on the cross so that your child could have life and life more abundantly. John recorded these words of Jesus: "I am come that they might have life, and that they might have it more abundantly" (John 10:10, KJV). He gave the gift of Himself to her. The apostle Paul wrote, "But God demonstrates his own love for us in this: While we were still sinners, Christ died for us" (Rom. 5:8, NIV). Because of Him, she can live forevermore. Because of Him, she can have joy unspeakable. Because of Him, her life on earth can have eternal significance. The blessings and treasures in Christ Jesus that are laid up for your child cannot be counted by man.

Your child is an integral part of God's overall plan for mankind. She is called to be a vessel through which truth and love will flow from God to other people. As you pray for and bless your child each day, keep in mind that God has a specific call upon her life. He has given her individual talents and gifts for her to use as she fulfills God's plan for her life. She is called according to the purposes of God to be part of a chosen people, a royal priesthood, a holy nation, a people belonging to God (1 Pet. 2:9). She is also set apart to fulfill a specific purpose as a part of the larger body of Christ. "For we are Gods workmanship, created in Christ Jesus to do good works, which God prepared in advance for us to do" (Eph. 2:10, NIV).

In the Book of Jeremiah, we see that the Lord knew your child before He formed her in the womb, and He set her apart before she was even born. "The word of the LORD came to me, saying, 'Before I formed you in the womb I knew you, before you were born I set you apart'" (Jer. 1:4–5, NIV). The Lord may begin to reveal to you some of the special characteristics and gifts He has already placed in your child. As He reveals to you insights about these unique qualities, you will have the wonderful opportunity of seeing how the hand of the Lord is upon your child in a very personal and individual way. Your role to train up your child in the way she should go will also become clearer. "Train up a child in the way he should go, and when he is old he will not turn from it" (Prov. 22:6, NIV).

There is much to celebrate, much reason to rejoice. As God's plans for your own life unfold, you will also be watching the Lord's workmanship and creation blossom into what He created your child to do. As your child gives

God pleasure in the days ahead, your own joy will become full. Your dedication to your child gives God great pleasure. Each day your expressions of faith in God, your love for Him and your tender care of your child are all purposes that He created you to do. "For it is God who works in you to will and to act according to his good purpose" (Phil. 2:13, NIV).

Day 1

MORNING

Sweet, precious one, I bless you. God made you a whole being; He formed you. I praise God because He made you in an amazing and wonderful way. What He has done is wonderful.

EVENING

I praise our heavenly Father who saw your bones being formed as you took shape in the womb. When you were put together there, He saw your body as it was formed. All the days planned for you were written in His book before you were one day old. The Father has wonderful plans for you.

Scripture Reading
Psalm 139:13–14, NCV
Psalm 139:15–16

Day 2

MORNING

Before the foundation of the world, the Father chose you to be His very own. His thoughts are precious toward you. They are so many! If I could count them, they would be more than all the grains of sand. He is with you when you are asleep and when you are awake.

EVENING

The Lord has examined you. He knows all about you. He knows when you sit down and when you get up. He knows your thoughts before you think them. He knows where you will go and where you will lie down. He knows thoroughly everything you will do. May He keep you under the protection of His wings.

Scripture Reading
Ephesians 1:3
Psalm 139:17, NCV
Psalm 139:1–3

MORNING

Even before you say a word, the Lord already knows it. He is all around you—in front and in back—and He has put His hand on you. His knowledge is amazing to me; it is more than I can understand. I thank the Lord for keeping you safe.

EVENING

If you climb to the sky, He is there! If you fly on morning's wings to the far, western horizon, He will find you in a minute—He will already be there waiting! You can know that He even sees you in the dark! At night you are immersed in the light!

Scripture Reading
Psalm 139:4–6, NCV
Psalm 139:7, THE MESSAGE

Day 4

MORNING

When you were being formed, God placed eternity in your heart. I pray and believe that you will do what is good. May you do what is right to other people and love being kind to others. Always obey God.

EVENING

Your real help in every situation comes from the Lord. His blessing will clothe you throughout your entire life.

Scripture Reading
Ecclesiastes 3:11, NIV
Micah 6:8, NCV
Psalm 3:8, The Message

Day 5

MORNING

By Christ Jesus, God created you to join in His work, the good work He has planned for you to do. May God be glorified through your life.

EVENING

My child, you were created for His good pleasure. May He continually create in you a new and clean heart that is filled with pure thoughts and right desires.

Scripture Reading
Ephesians 2:10
Psalm 51:10, TLB

MORNING

Jehovah created the heavens and earth and put everything, including you, in its place. He made the world to be lived in. You, sweet child, are in the world, but you are not of the world. May you always only speak truth and righteousness.

EVENING

May God bless you with a heart of faithfulness. May you understand that we are children of the same father, Abraham, all created by the same God. May He teach you what it means to be faithful to others and to keep the covenant of our spiritual fathers.

Scripture Reading
Isaiah 45:18
John 17:16
Malachi 2:10, TLB

Day 7

MORNING

I bless you, little one. I pray that you will be happy from the inside out and from the outside in—for you are firmly formed and loved.

EVENING

I bring you before the Lord. You are the work of His hands, of absolute truth and justice, faithful and right. All of His decrees and precepts are sure—fixed, established and trustworthy. May you always stand steadfast and remain established in Christ Jesus forever and ever.

Scripture Reading
Psalm 16:9, The Message
Psalm 111:7–8, AMP

Day 8

MORNING

I bless you, little one. With His very own hands God formed and fashioned you. Now I ask Him to breathe His wisdom over you so you can understand Him.

EVENING

Little one, I speak the Word of the Lord over you. He created you. He formed you. You do not have to be afraid because He has saved you. He has called you by name, and you are His.

Scripture Reading
Psalm 119:73, KJV, THE MESSAGE
Isaiah 43:1, NCV

Day 9

MORNING

The Lord said, "Bring to me all the people who are mine, whom I made for my glory, whom I formed and made." I now bring you before the Lord on this wondrous day, asking Him to bless you to follow paths of righteousness.

EVENING

God formed you for Himself that you might set forth His praise and sing songs to praise Him.

Scripture Reading
Isaiah 43:7
Isaiah 43:21, AMP, NCV

Day 10

MORNING

Little one, He who made you, who formed you in the womb and who will help you, says, "Do not be afraid."

EVENING

I bless you. Before God formed you in the womb He knew you, and before you were born He set you apart. He appointed you to tell about the wonderful acts of God. You were created for His pleasure.

Scripture Reading
Isaiah 44:2, NIV
Jeremiah 1:5, NIV
1 Peter 2:9

Day 11

MORNING

In the name of Jesus, I speak His word and bless you, our baby. It was God who made you. You are His! We are His people and the sheep of His pasture. Praise the name of the Lord!

EVENING

I thank God for pouring His Spirit upon you, my child, and His blessing upon our descendants. They shall spring up among the grass, as willows or poplars by the watercourses.

Scripture Reading
Psalm 100:3, AMP
Isaiah 44:3–4, AMP

MORNING

I thank God for giving me this precious gift. I am encouraged because you are important to God, and He takes care of you. He made you a little lower than the angels and crowned you with glory and honor. He is an awesome God!

EVENING

I bless you, ______, to know and understand His plan for your life. You belong to God. He put human beings in charge of everything that He made, and He put all things under their control. May He teach you to walk in this God-given authority and glorify His name.

Scripture Reading
Psalm 8:5, NCV
Psalm 8:6, NCV

Day 13

MORNING

Little one, the Lord has assigned you His portion and His cup; He has made your lot secure. May God make known to you the path of life, and fill you with joy in His presence and with eternal pleasures at His right hand.

EVENING

Once again I dedicate you to the Lord and to His service. Surely He will grant you eternal blessings and make you glad with the joy of His presence.

Scripture Reading
Psalm 16:5, 11, NIV
Psalm 21:6, NIV

Day 14

MORNING

Just as the Father took Jesus out of the womb, so He brought you forth out of the womb. May He teach you to trust even while you are on your mother's breast. I declare that He shall be your God, and you will not be far from Him.

EVENING

God knows you, our little one. When you call on the Lord, He will answer you and make you bold and stout-hearted.

Scripture Reading
Psalm 22:9, NKJV
Psalm 138:3, NIV

Day 15

MORNING

I bring you, our baby, before God. I thank our High God for you because you are breathtaking! Body and soul, you are marvelously made! I worship God in adoration over His creation! He made you inside and out.

EVENING

I rejoice in the works of His hands. God knows every bone in your body. He knows exactly how you were made, bit by bit, how you were sculpted from nothing into something.

Scripture Reading
Psalm 139:14, The Message
Psalm 139:15, The Message

MORNING

In all things God works for the good of those who love Him, who have been called according to His purpose. I thank God that He created you for His good pleasure.

EVENING

Nothing shall separate you, ______, from the love of Christ. Because of the way that Jesus our Master has embraced you, little one, absolutely *nothing* can come between you and God's love.

Scripture Reading
Romans 8:28, NIV
Romans 8:35, 39, NIV, THE MESSAGE

Day 17

MORNING

I pray that God's love will be at the center of your heart and that you will never fake it. I pray for God to give you the courage to run from evil and hold on for dear life to good. May you be a good friend who loves deeply and delights in honoring others.

EVENING

I love you, precious one. God gave you to me. I want you to grow up well and not be spoiled. Jesus is made unto us wisdom, and we will teach you His ways.

Scripture Reading
Romans 12:9, The Message, TLB
1 Corinthians 4:14, The Message

Day 18

MORNING

I believe that your body was made for God-given and God-modeled love, for "becoming one" with others who love Him.

EVENING

I pray that you will always respect your body as a sacred place, the place of the Holy Spirit. ______, you were bought with a price; therefore I pray that you will glorify God in your body and in your spirit, which are God's.

Scripture Reading
1 Corinthians 6:18, The Message
1 Corinthians 6:18–20, nkjv, The Message

Day 19

MORNING

I pray that you will be an imitator of God and walk in love. I ask the Lord to teach you to love others.

EVENING

I ask the Lord to teach you to walk as a child of light, for the fruit of the Spirit is in all goodness, righteousness and truth.

Scripture Reading
Ephesians 5:1–2, NCV
Ephesians 5:8

MORNING

I pray that God will teach you wisdom so that you may understand what the will of the Lord is. I also ask that honesty and integrity will be your virtue and protection.

EVENING

May you be granted with a calm, collected and circumspect attitude about life that you might obtain salvation through our Lord Jesus Christ.

Scripture Reading
Ephesians 5:15–17
Psalm 25:21
1 Thessalonians 5:6, AMP

Day 21

MORNING

I pray that you will be strong, courageous and firm throughout your life, and that God will be with you.

EVENING

May God give you a desire to do good, to be rich in good works and to be liberal, generous-hearted and ready to share with others.

Scripture Reading
Deuteronomy 31:6, AMP
1 Timothy 6:18, AMP

Day 22

MORNING

May the God of our Lord Jesus Christ, Father of glory, give you the spirit of wisdom and revelation in the knowledge of Him.

EVENING

I ask that God would grant to you, according to the riches of His glory, to be strengthened with might through His Spirit in your inner man.

Scripture Reading
Ephesians 1:17, NKJV
Ephesians 3:16

MORNING

May Christ dwell in your heart through faith. I ask the Father to teach you how to be rooted and grounded in love, and to be able to comprehend, with all the saints, what is the width, length, depth and height of the love of Christ, which passes knowledge, so that you may be filled with all the fullness of God.

EVENING

May God give you a desire to take refuge in Him and be glad; let you ever sing for joy. He will spread His protection over you so that you will love His name and rejoice in Him.

Scripture Reading
Ephesians 3:17
Psalm 5:11

Day 24

MORNING

I ask God to make known to you the path of life and to fill you with joy in His presence and with eternal pleasures at His right hand.

EVENING

May the Lord grant you the joy of His salvation and grant you a willing spirit to sustain you.

Scripture Reading
Psalm 16:11, NIV
Psalm 51:12, NIV

Day 25

MORNING

Jesus loves you even as the Father loves Him. May you ever remain in His love.

EVENING

I thank Jesus that you are well and whole. He has given you the gift of peace.

Scripture Reading
John 15:9
John 14:27, THE MESSAGE

Day 26

MORNING

May God grant you a daily walk of humility and gentleness. I pray for Him to help you to be patient, bearing with others in love.

EVENING

I thank God for choosing you for this new life of love. May you dress in the wardrobe He picked out for you: compassion, kindness, humility, quiet strength and discipline.

Scripture Reading
Ephesians 4:2, NIV
Colossians 3:12, The Message

Day 27

MORNING

May the Lord impart to you a strong desire to follow close behind Him, where you will be protected by His strong right arm.

EVENING

I ask God to help me teach you responsibility, for He has said that you must take responsibility for doing the creative best you can with your own life.

Scripture Reading
Psalm 63:8, TLB
Galatians 6:5, The Message

Day 28

MORNING

May God instill a desire in you to lovingly follow the truth at all times—that you may speak truly, deal truly, live truly—and so become more and more in every way like Christ who is the head of His body, the church.

EVENING

I know that God deserves honesty from the heart, yes, utter sincerity and truthfulness. May God give you this wisdom.

Scripture Reading
Ephesians 4:15, TLB
Psalm 51:6, TLB

Day 29

MORNING

May God grant you a glad heart and a joyful spirit. The Holy Spirit will teach you to pray unceasingly; no matter what happens, may you always be thankful.

EVENING

I pray that every detail in your life will be done in the name of the Master, Jesus, and that you will thank Father God every step of the way.

Scripture Reading
1 Thessalonians 5:16–18
Colossians 3:17, The Message

Day 30

MORNING

May you serve others wholeheartedly, as if you were serving the Lord, not men.

EVENING

Since such a great cloud of witnesses surrounds you, I pray for God to teach you to throw off everything that hinders and the sin that so easily entangles. Little one, run with perseverance the race marked out for you.

Scripture Reading
Ephesians 6:7, NIV
Hebrews 12:1, NIV

Day 31

MORNING

My prayer is that you will discover that God's Word is better than a diamond, better than a diamond set between emeralds. I pray that you will like it better than strawberries in spring, better than red, ripe strawberries.

EVENING

I pray that you will grow in the grace and knowledge of our Lord and Savior Jesus Christ. We give Him glory both now and forever! Amen.

Scripture Reading
Psalm 19:10, The Message
2 Peter 3:18, NIV

APRIL

Everything Is Beautiful

NEED TO PRAY

Because there are so many commands in the Bible for us to pray, it is impossible to be obedient to God if we do not have a life of prayer. Among the numerous scriptures that command us to pray are, "Pray continually; give thanks in all circumstances" (1 Thess. 5:17–18, NIV) and "Watch and pray" (Matt. 26:41, NIV).

Prayer is the gateway to blessing. "Ask and it will be given to you; seek and you will find; knock and the door will be opened to you. For everyone who asks receives; he who seeks finds; and to him who knocks, the door will be opened" (Matt. 7:7–8, NIV).

Prayer is needed for power, for intimacy with God and for protection against the power of the devil and temptations of this world. It brings fullness of joy and brings us into the realm of the heavenlies. When you pray, you can be confident that God will reveal to you more about His nature, give you revelation of truth that will guide you in your daily life and work on your behalf in sovereign and divine ways.

When you pray according to the Word of God, you are praying in accordance with the will of God, and He will hear you. Since the prayers and blessings in this book have been taken from the Word of God, you can be confident that you are praying according to the will of God for your child. "This is the confidence we have in approaching God: that if we ask anything according to his will, he hears us. And if we know that he hears us—whatever we ask—we know that we have what we asked of him" (1 John 5:14–15, NIV).

Because faith comes by hearing and hearing by the Word of God (Rom. 10:17), it naturally follows that praying and speaking blessings according to the Word of God will ignite faith in us. Faith is an essential component of answered prayer. "If you believe, you will receive whatever you ask for in prayer" (Matt. 21:22, NIV). "But let him ask in faith, nothing wavering" (James 1:6, KJV).

As you pray for your child, believe that those things that you are asking for in accordance with the Word of God will come to pass. You may not see the fulfillment of those prayers and words right now, but your faith will grow as you speak and hear the truth of God's Word. Just as the world was framed by the Word of God, your child's life will also be framed by His Word as you pray and speak words of blessing accordingly. "Faith is the substance of things hoped for, the evidence of things not seen. For by it the elders obtained a good report. Through faith we understand that the worlds were framed by the word of God, so that things which are seen were not made of things which do appear" (Heb. 11:1–3, KJV).

There are many examples in the Scriptures of parents praying for their children. One example is David's prayer for his son Solomon, when he asked the Lord, "And give my son Solomon the wholehearted devotion to keep your commands, requirements and decrees and to do everything to build the palatial structures for which I have provided" (1 Chron. 29:19, NIV). What more could we ask for our children than this? If our children will serve God with their whole hearts, they will surely have the abundant life that comes from having His presence in their lives.

A wholehearted love for God will result in wholehearted service and fulfillment of all of the commandments of God. "Jesus replied: 'Love the Lord your God will all your heart and with all your soul and with your mind.' This is the first and greatest commandment. And the second is like it: 'Love your neighbor as yourself.' All the Law and the Prophets hang on these two commandments" (Matt. 22:37–40, NIV).

Obedience to God and service to Him that is the result of love will bring forth fullness of blessings for our children. Their cup will truly run over with the fruits of their love and obedience that flow from Him. Praying for and blessing your child according to the Word and will of God, thereby pointing him to Jesus, is the greatest gift you could give him.

MORNING

I thank God for you, our beautiful child. I pray for God to enable you to see the wonder of your birth and your value to this family. He has made everything beautiful in its time.

EVENING

I thank God for the ending of a beautiful day. As I reflect back on the good things we have accomplished for His satisfaction and delight, I acknowledge that we are a happy and loving family because we are filled with His Gift.

Scripture Reading
Ecclesiastes 3:11–13, NIV
Ecclesiastes 3:11, NIV

MORNING

We awaken to a beautiful morning. By His Spirit, He will help us learn to recognize the power of His beauty in us so that we may do well. I am thankful to Him for His blessings, which make our lives rich today.

EVENING

I rejoice in the good that I have done for God today. You, my child, shall be a loving worker in Christ Jesus. The work of His hands is beautiful in His sight. We have lived for Him today.

Scripture Reading
Ecclesiastes 3:11–12, NIV
Proverbs 10:21, The Message
Ecclesiastes 3:13, NIV
Romans 16:3

Day 3

MORNING

My child, you have been made to live in beautiful dwelling places. I ask God to keep you safe, and I accept my responsibility for you. I ask God to send angels ahead of you to guard your way and bring you back to the place that He has prepared for you.

EVENING

As I look back on the events of this day, I know that I have been careful to obey His laws and that He has provided us with safety in the land. I thank God that we will dwell in the house of the Lord all the days of our lives, and we will gaze upon His beauty.

Scripture Reading
Genesis 43:9, NIV
Exodus 23:20, NIV
Leviticus 25:18, NIV
Proverbs 1:33, NIV
Psalm 27:4

MORNING

I arise to the beauty of another day. I purpose to train you in His ways, and you will not depart from them. God created you to be a beautiful person with self-respect, and you will learn to be respectful of others.

EVENING

As this day ends we revel in its beauty. I purpose not to exasperate you, my child, and I pray that you will receive instruction in the Lord.

Scripture Reading
Proverbs 22:6, NIV
Ephesians 6:2–4

Day 5

MORNING

God has a time for everything and a season for every activity under heaven. I pray that God will help set our priorities in order so that I am encouraged and can say that the Lord is our Helper.

EVENING

As I meditate on His Word tonight, I thank Him for a season flourishing with all sorts of good things. I am reminded that He has made everything beautiful in its time.

Scripture Reading

Ecclesiastes 3:6, NIV
Hebrews 13:5, NIV
Deuteronomy 6:7, NIV
Joshua 1:8, NIV
Ecclesiastes 3:1, NIV

Day 6

MORNING

I thank the Lord that He is with us. There is a time for emotional expression in our lives, and I acknowledge His intervention with joy. I thank God for blessing you, my child, with a good sense of humor.

EVENING

At the close of this day, we embrace one another in His love. I thank Him for being ever gracious to His children. We have hope in the risen Lion of Judah.

Scripture Reading
Luke 6:21, NIV
Ecclesiastes 3:4
Ecclesiastes 3:4–5
Isaiah 30:19
Revelation 5:5

Day 7

MORNING

A cheerful heart is a good medicine. I thank our heavenly Father that His Word abides in you this day so that you may respect others. May your words always be used to cheer up others.

EVENING

I thank Almighty God that He has allowed me to speak words of love to you today. As night has come, He has brought us to a comfortable silence. I thank God for you, little one. May the Lord use you to mend the hearts of other people.

Scripture Reading
Proverbs 17:22
Ecclesiastes 3:7

MORNING

God has made everything beautiful in its time. May He help you to always speak words of grace in all your conversations and guide you as you give answers to others.

EVENING

At the end of this day, I lift up praises to the Lord. May His praises continually be in your mouth, even at this time. It is beautiful tonight to be full of God. May you recognize that there is a time for everything.

Scripture Reading

Colossians 4:5, NIV
Psalm 34:1, NIV
Ecclesiastes 3:17, NIV

Day 9

MORNING

I thank God for everyone. I pray for those in authority over you, that you may live a peaceful and quiet life as you follow the Word of God and work to build unity between men.

EVENING

Sweet child, lie down in peace tonight, knowing that the heart of our leader is in the Lord's hand. To do what is right is more acceptable to the Lord than sacrifice. There is a time for war and a time for peace.

Scripture Reading
1 Timothy 2:1–3, NIV
2 Chronicles 30:12, NIV
Proverbs 21:1–3
Ecclesiastes 3:8

Day 10

MORNING

May God help you to be organized in your life. I ask for wisdom to enter your heart so that knowledge will be pleasant to your soul. I thank God for watching over His Word and keeping it.

EVENING

I rejoice in His salvation. May you have much time to reflect on Jesus and to be secure that you are saved along with this household. Young child, keep these thoughts near your heart, and toss away all fear.

Scripture Reading
Proverbs 2:10, NIV
Jeremiah 1:12, NIV
Acts 16:30

Day 11

MORNING

There is a time to be silent and a time to speak. I thank God that He will give you the peace of righteousness and its effect of quietness and confidence forever.

EVENING

I have great confidence that you will be all that God desires. He has prepared a way of safety, and He will protect you. He is your confidence. May we always rejoice in the beauty of our time together. He is our help.

Scripture Reading
Isaiah 30:15, NIV
Isaiah 32:17, NIV
2 Corinthians 7:4
Proverbs 3:26
Nehemiah 6:16, NIV

Day 12

MORNING

Come, my child, and listen while I give you lessons in worshiping God. Would you have a yearning for life? God has made this a beautiful day, and I look forward to the exciting beauty as it unfolds.

EVENING

See how good our God is! Be blessed, young child. Trust and take your refuge in Him. Reverence the Lord; worship Him. You will have no want if you truly revere and worship Him with a godly fear. I will train you in His ways.

Scripture Reading
Psalm 34:11–12, The Message
Psalm 34:8–9, AMP

Day 13

MORNING

This day I acknowledge the greatest mystery of all—Christ in us, the hope of glory. May this time together this morning plant seeds that will harvest the riches of salvation into the lives of those you meet, dear child.

EVENING

I uproot any unforgiveness that has seated itself in our spirits today and declare that it will not have any effect on you, my child. I forgive those who have sinned against me; therefore God shall forgive me. I hold this as God's promise. May God give you a heart that is quick to forgive.

Scripture Reading
Colossians 1:27, AMP
Matthew 6:14, NIV

Day 14

MORNING

Our dear child, always obey our God. I ask God to help you work out your salvation, for it is He who works in us to will and to act according to His good purpose.

EVENING

I petition God for the salvation of all those whom He has ordered for you to reach with the gospel during your lifetime. His salvation makes men's spirits beautiful in His time. I ask for repentance in their hearts so that they may be forgiven and come to the knowledge of God.

Scripture Reading
Philippians 2:12, NIV
1 Timothy 2:1, AMP

Day 15

MORNING

God has put great love in our hearts for one another. He has perfected and made us complete in Jesus. I purpose to walk in love individually and as a family so that we can bless others.

EVENING

There is a time for everything. As you grow closer to Him, may you grow in love for others. We take time right now to appreciate His love together.

Scripture Reading
Proverbs.17:17, NIV
Ecclesiastes 3:8

Day 16

MORNING

May you wait and hope in the Lord, holding firmly to your faith as you approach the throne of grace with confidence.

EVENING

You will be in places to receive the good news of the gospel. You will respect those who come to present His Word. You will worship the Lord in the splendor of His holiness. May He open your eyes to see the beauty of His time.

Scripture Reading
Psalm 130:5
Romans 10:15, NIV
1 Chronicles 16:29, NIV
Hebrews 4:14–16, NIV

MORNING

This morning I renew my vow to train you in the way of the Lord. I ask the Lord to cause you to retain His teaching forever. I know that whoever continues in the teaching has both the Father and the Son.

EVENING

His teachings have fallen like rain and His words like dew. Dear one, you are the tender plant that receives the rain. May God give you understanding so that you may meditate on His beautiful wonders.

Scripture Reading
2 John 9–10, NIV
Proverbs 22:6, NIV
Deuteronomy 32:2
Psalm 119:27

Day 18

MORNING

You will make a commitment to stand for God. He is able to make you stand firm in Him. I will declare that His love stands firm forever, that He established His faithfulness in heaven.

EVENING

I thank God for His loving-kindness that He brought to our family this day. He keeps His Word, and you are privileged to be included in His covenant. I will speak of His faithfulness and salvation to you, my child, and He will reveal His love and truth to you.

Scripture Reading
Romans 14:4
Psalm 89:2
Psalm 25:10
Psalm 40:10

Day 19

MORNING

God has blessed the places surrounding where you live. The trees of the field will yield fruit, and the ground will give crops. I thank God for your security.

EVENING

Lie down in peace this evening, dear child, because our dwelling place is secure. You can rest; you are secure in God. God has shielded you all day long. You can look about and rest in hope.

Scripture Reading
Ezekiel 34:26–28
Numbers 24:21
Deuteronomy 33:12
Job 11:18
Proverbs 14:26

Day 20

MORNING

My child, let's open our eyes to see the King in His beauty. I read this God-breathed Word and adhere to its teachings. The Father thoroughly equips you for every good work today.

EVENING

My child, let's rejoice in the beauty of our God! He has made everything beautiful in its time. Bask in God's love, and see the beauty in His creation. Acknowledge His plan and purpose for mankind.

Scripture Reading
2 Timothy 3:16, NIV
Isaiah 33:17, NIV
Ecclesiastes 3:11, NIV

Day 21

MORNING

May God make you a man (or woman) of knowledge who uses words with restraint. May you remain even-tempered in your relations with others. May no deceit be found in you.

EVENING

There is a time to be silent and a time to speak. May you know His time and purpose for everything. May you do what is right in the eyes of God and be a good example to others.

Scripture Reading
Proverbs17:27, NIV
Job 27:4, NIV
2 Corinthians 8:21

Day 22

MORNING

Praise to the King! His Word says that, "Children's children are the crown of old men, and the glory of children is their fathers." As I consider and give attention to care for and watch over you, I pray that our activities will stir up love and be helpful to your growth.

EVENING

I thank God for the love He has poured out into our hearts by the Holy Spirit. I ask God to fill your heart with His love. You will love God with all your heart, with all your soul and with all your mind. His love allows you to love others as you love yourself.

Scripture Reading
Proverbs 17:6, NIV
Hebrews 10:24, AMP
Romans 5:5, NIV
Matthew 22:37, NIV

Day 23

MORNING

I ask the Lord to teach you to love from a pure heart, from a good conscience and from unfeigned faith.

EVENING

May God help you to live a life of unfeigned faith that He has imparted as a gift to you and to me.

Scripture Reading
2 Timothy 1:5; 3:14–15

Day 24

MORNING

His Word is in our minds and hearts, and I purpose to teach them and impress them diligently upon your mind and heart, my child.

EVENING

I ask God to give you a hunger to know His Word. Together as a family, we will talk of His truth when we sit down or take a walk, when we lie down and when we rise up.

Scripture Reading
Deuteronomy 6:7

Day 25

MORNING

I thank God for granting consolation and joy to you, and for giving you an ornament of beauty, the oil of joy and a garment of praise.

EVENING

I thank God that you shall be called an oak of righteousness (lofty, strong and magnificent, distinguished for uprightness, justice and right standing with our God), the planting of the Lord, that He might be glorified.

Scripture Reading
Isaiah 61:3

Day 26

MORNING

I thank God for causing your steps to be firm and steadfast, immovable and always abounding in the work of the Lord.

EVENING

May God give you insight so that you will know and be continually aware that your labor in the Lord is not futile, never wasted or to no purpose.

Scripture Reading
1 Corinthians 15:58, AMP

Day 27

MORNING

Our beautiful baby, you belong to the household of faith, and you are God's true child according to a common faith.

EVENING

I bless you, my child, with grace, favor and spiritual blessing, and with a heart of peace from God the Father and the Lord Christ Jesus our Savior.

Scripture Reading
Titus 1:4

Day 28

MORNING

God knows the end from the beginning. I pray that everything you do in your life's work will be done in love, in a true love to God and man that is inspired by God's love for you.

EVENING

Little one, I speak God's Word over you and ask the Holy Spirit to always bring it to your remembrance. The Lord shall be to you an everlasting light in His glory and His beauty.

Scripture Reading
1 Corinthians 16:14, AMP
John 14:26
Isaiah 60:19, AMP

Day 29

MORNING

May you walk righteously and speak uprightly. As you do this, your eyes will see the King in His beauty, and they will behold a land of wide distances that stretches afar.

EVENING

God has abounded toward you in all wisdom and prudence. You will not be foolish, but you will look and consider well where you are going.

Scripture Reading
Isaiah 33:15, 17
Proverbs 14:15

Day 30

MORNING

You will grow up and offer yourself willingly in the day of His power, in the beauty of holiness and in holy array.

EVENING

When you are older, you will ascribe to Him glory and strength; you will give Him the glory due His name. You will bring an offering, come into His courts and worship Him in the beauty of holiness.

Scripture Reading
Psalm 110:3, AMP
Psalm 96:7–9, AMP

MAY

Character Building

May

THE POWER OF PRAISE

Along with blessing our children, we can also bless the Lord. We can do this by recognizing His characteristics, His sovereignty, His loving-kindness and His other attributes. An example of this can be found in Ephesians 1:3: "Blessed be the God and Father of our Lord Jesus Christ, who has blessed us with every spiritual blessing in the heavenly places in Christ" (NKJV). Just think of the magnitude of the blessing that is being spoken of here. It is important to note that when this scripture says, "has blessed us," it is referring to you and your young child. If you are living in Christ Jesus, the two of you are part of the word *us* in this scripture. Blessed be God, for you and your young child have been blessed with all spiritual blessings in heavenly places in Christ. Consider just how many blessings and words of faith you can speak over your child as you come into agreement with the Word of God!

When we praise God, we are acknowledging His perfection, works and benefits. Just how powerful is the act of praising God? Acts 16:25–34 gives an account of the power of praise to set free, deliver and bring about faith and salvation to others. "About midnight Paul and Silas were praying and singing hymns to God, and the other prisoners were listening to them. Suddenly there was such a violent earthquake that the foundations of the prison were shaken. At once all the prison doors flew open, and everybody's chains came loose" (vv.

25–26, NIV). Not only did their chains fall off, but when Paul and Silas spoke the word of the Lord to the jailer, "the jailer brought them into his house and set a meal before them; he was filled with joy because he had come to believe in God—he and his whole family" (v. 34, NIV). The power of praise will impact you and those around you.

Praises to God will fill your home and your heart in such a way that there is no room for despair and feelings of defeat. Instead of keeping our eyes fixed on our troubles and daily tasks, we turn our attention to praising our almighty King. He rules and reigns over every situation and over every task at hand. As we praise the Lord, joy springs forth in our hearts, and our strength is renewed. It may not be chains of iron that are broken; instead, it may be chains of worry or affliction. But just as the prayers and praises broke the chains of Paul and Silas, praying to God and praising Him will break our chains today, thereby enabling us to be a greater blessing to our child and to other people.

This book is a guidepost of daily blessings, prayers and expressions of praise and thanksgiving. While I encourage you to refer to and use this book at the beginning and end of each day, I also suggest that you fill your life and home with praises to God all day long: "Speaking to yourselves in psalms and hymns and spiritual songs, singing and making melody in your heart to the Lord" (Eph. 5:19, KJV). Let your child hear you singing songs of praise, lifting up your voice to the Lord in thanksgiving. Let him see the smile on your face and the gleam in your eye that comes from lifting your voice in praise to Him. "For the Lord is good; his mercy is everlasting; and his truth endureth to all generations" (Ps. 100:5, KJV). Yes, His truth endures to you and to the generations after you and after your child. His truth calls us to come to Him with thanksgiving and praise to bless His holy name.

Day 1

MORNING

______, I dedicate you for the work of the ministry, asking God to anoint you as a leader among men. You are a child sent to lead others to Jesus. I rejoice, knowing that the earth shall be full of the knowledge of the Lord as the waters cover the sea.

EVENING

May God grant you a love for justice and a desire to be to be fair, just, merciful and to walk humbly with your God.

Scripture Reading
Isaiah 11:6, 9, TLB
Psalm 11:7
Micah 6:8

Day 2

MORNING

I pray for God to help you to develop a strong self-esteem that is rooted in the realization that you are God's workmanship, created in Christ Jesus.

EVENING

May God open the eyes of your understanding so that you may know that God is sovereign over all. I ask God to give you a reverence for the life of God in others so that you may esteem and delight in them.

Scripture Reading
Ephesians 2:10
Ephesians 4:6; 5:2, AMP

Day 3

MORNING

May God bless you so that you may be strong and courageous! Then you will not be afraid!

EVENING

May God become your light! He makes any darkness bright.

Scripture Reading
Deuteronomy 31:6, TLB
2 Samuel 22:29, TLB

Day 4

MORNING

May God bless you with wise advisers. His plans will not fail.

EVENING

May you become a man (or woman) of understanding, drawing out the purposes of His heart.

Scripture Reading
Proverbs 15:22, NIV

MORNING

May God bless you to apply your heart to instruction and your ears to words of knowledge.

EVENING

I pray that you will have a heart to commit to the Lord whatever you do, and then your plans will succeed.

Scripture Reading
Proverbs 23:12, NIV
Proverbs 16:3, NIV

Day 6

MORNING

I pray that you will know skill, godly wisdom and instruction so that you may discern and comprehend the words of understanding and insight.

EVENING

I pray that you will receive instruction in dealing wisely, in the discipline of wise thoughtfulness, righteousness, justice and integrity.

Scripture Reading
Proverbs 1:1–3, AMP

MORNING

In your youth, may God give to you prudence, knowledge, discretion and discernment.

EVENING

May God grant you wisdom that you may hear and increase in learning. As a person of understanding, may you acquire skill and attend to sound counsel so that your course will be steered by God.

Scripture Reading
Proverbs 1:4–5, AMP

Day 8

MORNING

By the grace of God, may you be made to understand a proverb and a figure of speech, or an enigma with its interpretation, and the words of the wise and their sayings or riddles.

EVENING

May God create in you a reverent and worshipful fear of the Lord, for this is the beginning, the principal and the choice part of knowledge.

Scripture Reading
Proverbs 1:6–7, AMP

Day 9

MORNING

I pray that you will hearken to Wisdom so that you may dwell securely, in confident trust and in quietness without fear or dread of evil.

EVENING

I bless you with a desire for insight so that you may raise your voice for understanding, seek for wisdom as silver and search for skillful and godly wisdom as for hidden treasures.

Scripture Reading
Proverbs 1:33, AMP
Proverbs 2:3–4, AMP

MORNING

May God grant you an understanding of the reverent and worshipful fear of the Lord so that you may find the knowledge of our omniscient God.

EVENING

May you be blessed to pick out what is true and fair, and find all the good trails! I pray that Lady Wisdom will be your close friend, and Brother Knowledge your pleasant companion.

Scripture Reading
Proverbs 2:5, AMP
Proverbs 2:9–10, The Message

Day 11

MORNING

May you be blessed with true companions. I pray that Good Sense will scout ahead for danger and that Insight will keep an eye out for you, keeping you from making wrong turns or following the bad directions.

EVENING

May God give you a desire to follow the steps of the godly and stay on the right path, for men of integrity who are blameless and complete in God's sight shall enjoy fullness of life.

Scripture Reading
Proverbs 2:11–12, THE MESSAGE
Proverbs 2:20–21, AMP, TLB

Day 12

MORNING

I pray that you will trust God from the bottom of your heart.

EVENING

May you always listen for God's voice in everything you do and everywhere you go. I trust the Lord to keep you on track.

Scripture Reading
Proverbs 3:5–6, THE MESSAGE

Day 13

MORNING

May you honor the Lord with your wealth, with the first fruits of all of your crops.

EVENING

I pray that you will never tire of loyalty and kindness, and ask that you hold these virtues tightly and write them deep within your heart.

Scripture Reading
Proverbs 3:9, NIV
Proverbs 3:2–3, TLB

Day 14

MORNING

I ask God to keep you free of conceit. Instead, may you ever trust and reverence the Lord, and may you turn your back on evil.

EVENING

May the Lord bless you to know right from wrong, and may you have good judgment and common sense.

Scripture Reading
Proverbs 3:7, TLB
Proverbs 3:21, TLB

Day 15

MORNING

I pray that your goals will be to know and do right, and to have common sense. May you not let them slip away, for they will fill you with living energy and bring you honor and respect.

EVENING

May you always acknowledge that the Lord is your confidence and that He shall keep your foot from being caught.

Scripture Reading
Proverbs 3:22, TLB
Proverbs 3:26, NAS

Day 16

MORNING

Here I am again on this beautiful morning with the child whom the Lord has given to our family. I pray that we will be for signs and wonders to this generation, and glorify Him in all that we do.

EVENING

I receive God's promise on your behalf. His Holy Spirit shall not leave you, and you shall want the good and hate the wrong.

Scripture Reading
Isaiah 59:21, TLB

MORNING

May the Lord impart to you a desire to do good to those who deserve it when it is in your power to act.

EVENING

May you be blessed with integrity so that you may fulfill your obligations as a citizen. I pray for God to instill in you a desire to pay your taxes, pay your bills and respect your leaders.

Scripture Reading

Proverbs 3:27, NIV
Isaiah 8:18, NKJV
Romans 13:7, THE MESSAGE

Day 18

MORNING

I praise God, believing that every time you get the chance, you will work for the benefit of all, starting with the people closest to you in the community of faith.

EVENING

I thank God for declaring our home blessed—joyful and favored with blessings. May I be a blessing to you, our baby, as I nurture you in the ways of the Lord.

Scripture Reading
Galatians 6:10, THE MESSAGE
Proverbs 3:33, AMP

Day 19

MORNING

I declare that the Lord blesses you and that you shall inherit the earth.

EVENING

May God impart to you the wisdom to live wisely. I thank God that wise living is rewarded with honor.

Scripture Reading
Psalm 37:22, TLB
Proverbs 3:35, The Message

Day 20

MORNING

I pray that you will hear the instruction of your earthly father and your heavenly Father, and that you will pay attention in order to gain and to know intelligent discernment, comprehension and interpretation of spiritual matters.

EVENING

I pray to the Lord God of Hosts that your heart will hold fast the words of truth and that you will keep His commandments and live.

Scripture Reading
Proverbs 4:1, AMP
Proverbs 4:4, AMP

MORNING

May God open the eyes of your understanding so that you may know Him in a personal way; be acquainted with and understand Him; and appreciate, heed and cherish Him.

EVENING

I pray that you will serve God with a blameless heart and a willing mind. Find comfort in knowing that He searches all hearts and minds and understands all the wanderings of the thoughts. May His will be done in your life on earth as it is in heaven.

Scripture Reading
1 Chronicles 28:9, AMP
Matthew 6:10

Day 22

MORNING

May God create in you a desire to prize Wisdom highly and exalt her. She will exalt and promote you and will bring you to honor when you embrace her.

EVENING

May God give you the hearing to receive His sayings, and the years of your life shall be many.

Scripture Reading
Proverbs 4:8–10, AMP

Day 23

MORNING

I ask God to give you comprehensive insight into His ways and purposes and to lead you in paths of uprightness. When you walk, your steps shall not be hampered; when you run, you shall not stumble.

EVENING

May your path be like the light of dawn that shines brighter and clearer until it reaches its full strength and glory in the perfect day that is prepared.

Scripture Reading
Proverbs 4:11–12, AMP
Proverbs 4:18, AMP

Day 24

MORNING

May God grant you the ability to concentrate and pay attention to His words so that you may consent and submit to His sayings. May they not depart from your sight, but may you keep them in the center of your heart.

EVENING

Little one, I bless you with eyes that look right ahead, with fixed purpose, as you consider well the path of your feet. I pray that all your ways will be established and ordered aright by Him.

Scripture Reading
Proverbs 4:20–21, AMP
Proverbs 4:25–26, AMP

Day 25

MORNING

I ask the Lord to grant you the ability to pay attention to our wisdom and listen well to our words of insight so that you may maintain discretion and your lips preserve knowledge.

EVENING

I pray that when you marry, you will confine yourself to your own spouse, and your children shall be for the two of you alone.

Scripture Reading
Proverbs 5:1–2, NIV
Proverbs 5:17, AMP

Day 26

MORNING

I pray that you will be blessed with the rewards of fidelity, and that you will rejoice in the spouse of your youth.

EVENING

Little one, our ways are directly before His eyes, and He, who would have us to live soberly, chastely and godly, carefully weighs all men's goings.

Scripture Reading
Proverbs 5:18–21, AMP

Day 27

MORNING

I ask the Holy Spirit to help you to follow your father's good advice. May you never wander off from your mother's teachings.

EVENING

At the close of another day, I pray that you will wrap yourself in good advice and sound teaching from head to foot, wearing them like a scarf around your neck.

Scripture Reading
Proverbs 6:20–21, The Message

Day 28

MORNING

I pray that where you walk, good advice and sound teachings will guide you; whenever you rest, they will guard you; and when you wake up, they will tell you what lies ahead.

EVENING

I thank God that you welcome and receive sound advice, for it is a beacon. Good teaching is a light, and moral discipline is a life path for you.

Scripture Reading
Proverbs 6:22–23, The Message

MORNING

I bless you, my child, to keep our words. Lay up within you our commandments for use when they are needed, and may you always treasure them.

EVENING

I affirm that you will keep His commandments and live, and keep His teaching as the apple (the pupil) of your eye. The Holy Spirit will help you bind them on your fingers and write them on the tablet of your heart.

Scripture Reading
Proverbs 7:1–3

Day 30

MORNING

I ask God to help me to be a good example to you. Then you will speak excellent and princely things, and the opening of your lips shall be for right things.

EVENING

I pray that all the words of your mouth will be righteous, upright and in right standing with God.

Scripture Reading
Proverbs 8:7–8, AMP

Day 31

MORNING

May God give to you an open mind so that you will recognize truth.

EVENING

May God instruct me so that I might teach you that skillful and godly wisdom is better than rubies or pearls, and all the things that may be desired are not to be compared to it.

Scripture Reading
Proverbs 8:9, The Message
Proverbs 8:11, AMP

JUNE

The Lord Keeps Watch

June

GIVE THANKS

Praising God and thanking Him are certainly closely related, but when we express thanksgiving to God, we are often thanking Him for specific blessings from which we have benefited.

How often do we ask God for one thing after another, yet forget to thank Him for what He has already provided us? In Paul's letter to Philemon we see a wonderful example of combining prayer with giving thanks to God. Paul wrote Philemon, "I always thank my God as I remember you in my prayers" (v. 4, NIV). This is a wonderful example of how our thanksgiving to God should be expressed to Him when we intercede in prayer for other people.

So often the Lord blesses us abundantly, yet we don't approach Him with an attitude of thankfulness before we begin to ask Him for something else. However, if we stop to meditate on the grace, mercy and love of the majestic Ruler we serve, we begin to understand how His very nature calls us to enter into His presence with thanksgiving and praise. He is King eternal, the God of Hosts, the Most High, the Living God! Thankfulness will be ignited in us when we begin to consider the wonder and splendor of the mighty King whose throne is heaven and whose footstool is earth. This glorious King, our mighty God who communes with us, is not only the ruler of the universe, but He is also concerned about everything that concerns us. He even knows the number of hairs that are on our heads. Is it any wonder that the Scriptures give us the pattern of how we should approach our King as described in Psalm 100:4? "Enter into his gates with thanksgiving, and into his courts with praise: be thankful unto him, and bless his name" (KJV). In Psalm 95:2 we are told, "Let us come before him with thanksgiving and extol him with music and song" (NIV).

Should our prayers always be accompanied by thanksgiving? Yes. In fact, Philippians 4:6 tells us that our requests in prayer must be accompanied by thanksgiving. "But in everything by prayer and supplication, with thanksgiving, let your requests be made known to God" (NKJV). Further confirmation of this is given in Colossians 4:2: "Devote yourselves to prayer, being watchful and thankful" (NIV). So not only are we to pray and be thankful, but we are to be devoted to it.

In his prayer in 1 Chronicles 29:10–13, David exalts the Lord, recognizing that blessings come from Him and thanking Him.

> Praise be to you, O LORD,
> God of our father Israel,
> from everlasting to everlasting.
> Yours, O LORD, is the greatness and the power
> and the glory and the majesty and the splendor,
> for everything in heaven and earth is yours.
> Yours, O LORD, is the kingdom;
> you are exalted as head over all.
> Wealth and honor come from you;
> you are the ruler of all things.

In your hands are strength and power
to exalt and give strength to all.
Now, our God, we give you thanks,
and praise your glorious name.

—NIV

We have so much for which to be thankful. In fact, everything wonderful around us comes from Him. The gift of eternal life through our Lord and Savior Jesus Christ comes from Him. The beauties we behold, the laughter, the warmth, the comfort we find in family and friends, the sorrows that shape our character, the bounty of His creation—all these and so much more come from Him. Yes, even the child you hold close to your heart comes from Him. Everything, absolutely everything, good comes from Him. "Every good gift and every perfect gift is from above, and comes down from the Father of lights, with whom there is no variation or shadow of turning" (James 1:17, NKJV).

So give God thanks. Thank Him for what He has already has done. Dedicate yourself and your child wholly to Him, and thank Him for the promises He is about to fulfill in your lives.

Day 1

MORNING

I pray that our Father God will always shield you, our precious baby, on all sides and give you courage. I am thankful that God hears our prayers as we begin this new day.

EVENING

As we prepare to go to bed, I take time to be still with you, my child, and think about our God and His Son, Jesus. Together as a family, we rejoice because God will be exalted among the nations; He will be exalted in the earth. Father God, we exalt You in our home!

Scripture Reading
Psalm 3:3, NCV
Psalm 46:10

MORNING

I believe that you, our baby, are marked for God's kingdom. I know that He will bless you, for surely He blesses the righteous. He will surround you with His favor as with a shield.

EVENING

I thank God for being a strength and shield to you. Your heart shall trust in the Lord, and you will be helped. Your heart will leap for joy, and you will give thanks to Him in song.

Scripture Readings
Psalm 5:12, NIV
Psalm 28:7

Day 3

MORNING

The Lord is your fort where you can enter and be safe. He is a rugged mountain where you can hide. He is your Savior, a rock where none can reach you and a tower of safety.

EVENING

I ask God, our Father, to protect you as He would His own eye and to hide you in the shadow of His wings.

Scripture Reading
Psalm 18:2, TLB
Psalm 17:8, NCV

Day 4

MORNING

Here in the stillness of the morning I am quiet, and I come to you prayerfully. We rest in the Lord, and wait patiently for Him. As you, our little one, grow into adulthood, may you look to the Lord and not be bothered with those who try to elbow their own way to the top of the ladder.

EVENING

May Father God give you the desires of your heart as you delight yourself in Him.

Scripture Reading
Psalm 37:7, NKJV, THE MESSAGE
Psalm 37:4, NKJV

MORNING

I thank the Lord for this day that He has made. Little one, the angels are at His command, and He will command His angels concerning you, to guard you in all your ways.

EVENING

I thank God that you will receive His salvation. He has sent out His angels, who are spirit-messengers, to help care for you.

Scripture Reading
Psalm 91:11, NIV
Hebrews 1:14, TLB

Day 6

MORNING

May Father God wake you each morning with the sound of His loving voice; then you will go to sleep each night trusting in Him. He will point out the road you must travel.

EVENING

______, you shall lie down and sleep in peace and wake up safely, for the Lord is watching over you.

Scripture Reading
Psalm 143:8, The Message
Psalm 3:5, TLB

Day 7

MORNING

I pray that you will experience for yourself the truth, and the truth will free you.

EVENING

I thank God that you will lie down and sleep in peace, for the Lord alone makes you dwell in safety.

Scripture Reading
John 8:32, THE MESSAGE
Psalm 4:8, NIV

MORNING

I pray that as you go out into the outside world, the Lord Jesus will help you watch out for doomsday deceivers.

EVENING

Because He watches over Israel, and He neither slumbers nor sleeps, He will watch over you. God loves you, ______, and I thank Him for it.

Scripture Reading
Matthew 24:4, The Message
Psalm 121:4, NIV

Day 9

MORNING

I thank God that you will keep our commands, and you will not forsake the law of your mother. Wherever you walk, they will guide you; whenever you rest, they will guard you; when you wake up, they will tell you what's next.

EVENING

When you lie down, you will not be afraid; when you lie down, you will sleep in peace.

Scripture Reading
Proverbs 6:22, The Message
Proverbs 3:24, NCV

Day 10

MORNING

I honor our Father in heaven, and I honor His holy name. May His kingdom come now. May His will be done here on earth in your life, just as it is in heaven.

EVENING

May the Holy Spirit, anoint your ears to hear the words of Jesus and give you the desire to put them into practice. You will be like a wise man (or woman) who builds his (or her) house on the rock. Though the floods may come and the winds may blow, your house will stand.

Scripture Reading
Matthew 6:9–10, TLB
Matthew 7:24, NIV

Day 11

MORNING

May the heavenly Father reveal to you just as He did to Simon Peter that Jesus is the Christ, the Messiah, the Son of the living God.

EVENING

May you follow the Lord always. When you call, He will answer, and He will make you a fisherman for the souls of men!

Scripture Reading
Matthew 16:16, The Message
Mark 1:17, TLB

Day 12

MORNING

May you love the Lord God with all your passion, prayer, intelligence and energy, and may you love others as well as you love yourself.

EVENING

Always remember the care and attention your heavenly Father gives to every last detail that concerns you, and never be intimidated by other people The very hairs on your head are numbered by the Lord.

Scripture Reading
Mark 12:30–31, The Message
Luke 12:6–7, The Message

Day 13

MORNING

May you learn how necessary it is for you to pray consistently and never quit.

EVENING

______, God loves you so much that He gave His one and only Son, that when you believe in Him, you shall not perish but have eternal life.

Scripture Reading
Luke 18:1, THE MESSAGE
John 3:16, NIV

Day 14

MORNING

______, Jesus came that you might have life, and that you might have it more abundantly.

EVENING

May the Father give you the revealed knowledge that Jesus is the way, the truth and the life, and that no one comes to the Father except through Him.

Scripture Reading
John 10:10
John 14:6

Day 15

MORNING

May the Holy Spirit give you the understanding that Jesus is the vine and you are the branch. If you are in Him, you will bear much fruit.

EVENING

Jesus told us these things so that you may have peace. In this world you will have trouble, but take heart: He has overcome the world.

Scripture Reading
John 15:5, NIV
John 16:33, NIV

Day 16

MORNING

I thank the Father for the written Word. John wrote down His gospel so that you will believe that Jesus is the Messiah, the Son of God. In the act of believing, you will have real and eternal life.

EVENING

I thank God for pouring out His Spirit on all flesh. ______, you are one of His sons and daughters, and you shall prophesy.

Scripture Reading
John 20:31, The Message
Acts 2:16–18, NKJV

Day 17

MORNING

I pray that when the time arrives, you will repent and be baptized in the name of Jesus Christ for the remission of sins, and you will receive the gift of the Holy Spirit.

EVENING

May His Spirit fall on you when you hear His Word.

Scripture Reading
Acts 2:38, NKJV
Acts 10:44, NKJV

Day 18

MORNING

May you be a happy disciple of the Lord Jesus Christ, brimming with joy and the Holy Spirit.

EVENING

I pray that you and your household will believe on the Lord Jesus Christ and be saved when you are an adult living in your own home.

Scripture Reading
Acts 13:52, The Message
Acts 16:31, NKJV

Day 19

MORNING

______, you are God's offspring. In Him, you live, move and have your being.

EVENING

May you be most proud to proclaim this extraordinary message of God's powerful plan to rescue everyone who trusts Him, starting with Jews and then to everyone else!

Scripture Reading
Acts 17:28, NIV
Romans 1:16, THE MESSAGE

MORNING

May your love always be real. I pray that you will hate what is evil, and hold on to what is good.

EVENING

I bless you, my child, and believe that you will rely on all the energy you receive from God Himself to get along with others. You will help others with encouraging words.

Scripture Reading
Romans 12:9, NCV
Romans 14:19, THE MESSAGE

Day 21

MORNING

______, you have free and open access to God, given by Jesus.

EVENING

______, your body is the temple of the Holy Spirit; you are not your own.

Scripture Reading
1 Corinthians 1:4, THE MESSAGE
1 Corinthians 6:19, NKJV

Day 22

MORNING

I know that no test or temptation that comes your way will be beyond the course of what others have to face. May you always remember that He will never let you down; He will always be there to help you come through it.

EVENING

I pray that you will walk in the kind of love that bears all things, believes all things, hopes all things and endures all things. This kind of love will never fail.

Scripture Reading
1 Corinthians 10:13
1 Corinthians 13:7–8

Day 23

MORNING

I pray that you will keep your eyes open for spiritual danger, stand true to the Lord, act like a godly man (or woman) and be strong. In all that you do, may you do it with kindness and love.

EVENING

I thank the Lord that you will have no veil over your face; you can be a mirror that brightly reflects the glory of the Lord. As the Spirit of the Lord works within you, you will become more and more like Him.

Scripture Reading
1 Corinthians 16:13–14, TLB
2 Corinthians 3:18, TLB

Day 24

MORNING

______, I bless you to speak truth at all times. The Lord will set a guard over your mouth and keep watch over the door of your lips.

EVENING

Tonight I bless you with the desire to practice the presence of Jesus and keep watch with Him.

Scripture Reading
Psalm 141:3, NIV
Matthew 26:40, NIV

Day 25

MORNING

When you, ______, receive Jesus as your Lord, you will become a brand-new person inside. You will not be the same any longer. A new life begins!

EVENING

I pray that you will not be teamed with those who do not love the Lord, for what do the people of God have in common with the people of sin? How can light live with darkness?

Scripture Reading
2 Corinthians 5:17, TLB
2 Corinthians 6:14, TLB

MORNING

Before the Father, I bless you, our son (or daughter) with grace and peace from God our Father and the Lord Jesus Christ. I thank Jesus for giving Himself for our sins to rescue you from the present evil age, according to the will of our God and Father.

EVENING

I thank God for giving you, my child, freedom—not freedom to do wrong, but freedom to love and serve others.

Scripture Reading
Galatians 1:3–4, NIV
Galatians 5:13, TLB

Day 27

MORNING

May you never get fatigued doing good, for at the right time you will harvest a good crop if you don't give up or quit.

EVENING

I thank God for blessing me with you. I ask the God of our Master, Jesus Christ, the God of glory, to make you intelligent and discerning in knowing Him personally.

Scripture Reading
Galatians 6:9, The Message
Ephesians 1:17, The Message

Day 28

MORNING

May your eyes be focused and clear, so that you can see exactly what the Lord is calling you to do. I bless you so that you might grasp the immensity of this glorious way of life He has for His children.

EVENING

I pray that you will be kind to others, tender-hearted, forgiving others, just as God in Christ also forgave you.

Scripture Reading
Ephesians 1:18, The Message
Ephesians 4:32

Day 29

MORNING

Our prayer this morning is that you will not live carelessly or unthinkingly. I ask God to grant you the wisdom to understand what the Master wants of you.

EVENING

May you be strong in the Lord and in His mighty power and have the desire to put on the full armor of God so that you can take your stand against the devil's schemes.

Scripture Reading
Ephesians 5:17, The Message
Ephesians 6:10–11, NIV

Day 30

MORNING

This morning I affirm and have no doubt in my mind that He who started this great work in you will continue it and bring it to a flourishing finish on the very day Christ Jesus appears.

EVENING

I thank God for His peace that garrisons and mounts guard over your heart and mind through Christ Jesus as you prepare to go to sleep.

Scripture Reading
Philippians 1:6, THE MESSAGE
Philippians 4:7, AMP
1 Corinthians 16:13–14, NKJV

JULY

Peace That Passes Understanding

July

THE TONGUE MUST BE BRIDLED

Now is the time to choose the type of environment in which your child will grow. Will he grow up hearing praises and blessings, or will he have to cringe to the sound of cursing? There are many forms of cursing, all of which are destructive and hurtful. Daily we are faced with choices to either bless or curse, to bridle our tongue or to open the gateway of destruction. Like David, the prayer of hearts must be, "May the words of my mouth and the meditation of my heart be pleasing in your sight, O LORD, my Rock and my Redeemer" (Ps. 19:14, NIV).

Our prayer each day should also be, "Set a watch, O LORD, before my mouth: keep the door of my lips" (Ps. 141:3, KJV). Imagine a home where a child is never called an ugly name and never hears gossip, complaining, arguing, hurtful accusations, words of doubt, malice, guile, self-condemnation, lying, cheating, selfishness, pride or filthiness! You may ask yourself, "Is this possible?" The answer to that question lies in the scripture, "Do not let any unwholesome talk come out of your mouths, but only what is helpful for building others up according to their needs, that it may benefit those who listen" (Eph. 4:29, NIV).

Out of the same mouth can come both blessings and cursing, but this should not be the case. If we have decided to bless our children in accordance with the Word of God, then it is important for us to be consistent. We must not bless them one minute and curse them in anger the next. We must not praise God, only to then turn around and speak accusations and complaints against Him or members of the family of believers. "With the tongue we praise our Lord and Father, and with it we curse men, who have been made in God's likeness. Out of the same mouth come praise and cursing. My brothers, this should not be" (James 3:9–10, NIV).

The principle of sowing and reaping applies to the words we speak. Though it will take self-discipline, if we seek God's wisdom and rely on Him to help us maintain an environment of blessings and praises to God, the harvest will be great. "Let us not become weary in doing good, for at the proper time we will reap a harvest if we do not give up. Therefore, as we have opportunity, let us do good to all people, especially to those who belong to the family of believers" (Gal. 6:9–10, NIV).

If we rejoice in all things, even during times of difficulty, then our gentleness will be evident to everyone around us, including our own children. Rather than relying on our own strength and becoming anxious, we can do the very opposite of that by presenting our requests to God through prayer and thanksgiving. The end result will be that the peace of God, which transcends all understanding, will guard our hearts and our minds in Christ Jesus (Phil. 4:4–7). To bridle the tongue we must also bridle the mind. What we choose to think about will guide our actions, reactions and words. In fact, Philippians 4:8 tells us exactly what to think about: "Finally, brothers, whatever is true, whatever is noble, whatever is right, whatever is pure, whatever is lovely, whatever is admirable—if anything is excellent or praiseworthy—think about such things" (NIV).

Praise God for the wonderful child He has given you. God has wonderful plans for him and for you. "However, as it is written: 'No eye has seen, no ear has heard, no mind has conceived what God has prepared for those who love him'—but God has revealed it to us by his Spirit" (1 Cor. 2:9, NIV). Ask God for wisdom for you to understand what He has prepared for you and your child in Christ Jesus. To the natural mind, His plans are incomprehensible, but by His Spirit the Lord will give you understanding and bold confidence as you put on the mind of Christ.

Day 1

MORNING

I bless you, precious one whom God has sent to me. I thank God for sending you a special Friend, the Holy Spirit, who will make everything plain to you. I thank Jesus for keeping you well and whole. He has given you a beautiful parting gift: peace.

EVENING

I thank the Father for another day of peace. Little one, our Lord God has given you peace, and you will go to sleep without fear. He will chase away all adversity.

Scripture Reading
John 14:26–27, The Message
Leviticus 26:6, TLB

Day 2

MORNING

The Lord bless you and keep you, little one; the Lord make His face shine upon you and be gracious to you; the Lord turn His face toward you and give you peace.

EVENING

Just as Gideon did, I build an altar here in our hearts and name it "The Altar of Peace With Jehovah." I thank God that you, my child, enjoy the peace and harmony of our home.

Scripture Reading
Numbers 6:24–26, NIV
Judges 6:24, TLB

Day 3

MORNING

I thank God that the peace He promised to David and his descendants will be on our household and on our descendants after us.

EVENING

May the Lord grant you the will to listen carefully to all He is saying—for He speaks peace to you. I pray that you will choose to do good.

Scripture Reading
1 Kings 2:33, NIV
Psalm 85:8, TLB

Day 4

MORNING

His Word declares that mercy and truth have met together. Righteousness and peace have kissed! Truth rises from the earth, and righteousness smiles down from heaven. I thank the Lord for His blessings that He will pour down on you.

EVENING

May the Lord grant you a love for His laws. You will have great peace of heart and mind, and you will not stumble.

Scripture Reading
Psalm 85:10–12, TLB
Psalm 119:165, TLB

Day 5

MORNING

I confess that Jesus is Lord of our family. I ask Him to open your eyes that you may know Jesus as "Wonderful," "Counselor," "The Mighty God," "The Everlasting Father," "The Prince of Peace."

EVENING

May you learn to trust in the Lord forever and have a steadfast mind. He will keep you in perfect peace.

Scripture Reading
Isaiah 9:6, TLB
Isaiah 26:3–4, NIV

Day 6

MORNING

I pray that you will walk in paths of righteousness, for the fruit of righteousness will be peace; the effect of righteousness will be quietness and confidence forever.

EVENING

I thank the Father that we are His people, and you, our precious child, will live in a peaceful dwelling place, in a secure home, in an undisturbed place of rest.

Scripture Reading
Isaiah 32:17–18, NIV

Day 7

MORNING

I acknowledge that God has entrusted you to our care, and I pray that you will listen to His laws! Then you will have peace flowing like a gentle river, and great waves of righteousness.

EVENING

Before our heavenly Father, I bless you tonight. I pray that you will not fear or be dismayed as you fulfill your destiny. You and your descendants will have peace and security, and no one will make you afraid, for God is with you.

Scripture Reading
Isaiah 48:18–19, TLB
Jeremiah 30:10, NIV

Day 8

MORNING

I enter into the covenant of peace God made with His children, an everlasting pact. I thank God for blessing you and future generations. The Lord God has made His home among us. He is our God, and we are His people.

EVENING

I acknowledge and praise the One who will stand and shepherd His flock in the strength of the Lord, in the majesty of the name of the Lord God. You, my child, will live securely. Jesus is your peace.

Scripture Reading
Ezekiel 37:26–27, TLB
Micah 5:4–5, NIV
Ephesians 2:14

Day 9

MORNING

Note to parents: Your child will learn to pray for others by the example you set before him. This is a prayer of intercession for all nations.

Father, I come before you this morning praying for the world in which my child lives. I pray that in his (or her) lifetime you will bring peace among the nations. God's dominion shall stretch from sea to sea, from the river to the ends of the earth.

EVENING

Through the heartfelt mercies of our God, God's Sunrise will break in upon you, shining on you even if you are in the darkness. Then God's Sunrise will show you the way, one foot at a time, down the path of peace.

Scripture Reading
Zechariah 9:10, NKJV
Luke 1:78–79, THE MESSAGE

Day 10

MORNING

I thank God for His peace that He left with us—the peace He gave to you. I pray that you will not let your heart be troubled and that you will not be afraid as you pursue the more abundant life.

EVENING

May Father God grant you spiritual understanding. I pray that you will follow after the Holy Spirit, for that will lead you to life and peace.

Scripture Reading
John 14:27, NIV
Romans 8:6, TLB

Day 11

MORNING

May God open the eyes of your understanding. May your feet be fitted with the readiness that comes from the gospel of peace.

EVENING

In the name of Jesus, I loose your mind from thoughts of fretting and anxiety. I bind you to God's peace, which transcends all understanding. May this peace guard your heart and mind in Christ Jesus.

Scripture Reading

Ephesians 6:15, NIV
Matthew 18:18
Philippians 4:7, NIV

Day 12

MORNING

God the Father has His eye on you and has determined to keep you obedient by the work of the Spirit through the sacrifice of Jesus. May everything good from God be yours! Grace and peace be yours in abundance.

EVENING

______, Jesus gave us the keys of the kingdom of heaven. Whatever we bind on earth will be bound in heaven, and whatever we loose on earth will be loosed in heaven. I bind your spirit, soul and body to the peace of God.

Scripture Reading
1 Peter 1:2, NIV, THE MESSAGE
Matthew 16:19, NKJV

Day 13

MORNING

May the Lord be gracious to you, ______, and give you a heart that longs for Him. May He be your strength every morning, and your salvation in time of distress.

Note to parents: The following prayer is one that I heard my father pray each night just before bedtime. He has continued to pray this for his family throughout his lifetime. This prayer was my consolation in times of distress and delivered me from many fears.

EVENING

I bow my knee to the Father of our Lord Jesus Christ. We can lie down in peace and sleep, knowing that the angel of the Lord encamps around about our home and keeps us safe.

Scripture Reading
Isaiah 33:2, NIV
Ephesians 3:14, NKJV
Psalm 34:7, NIV

Day 14

MORNING

May you love all that God reveals to you. You will not stumble around in the dark.

EVENING

When you lie down, you will not be afraid; when you lie down, your sleep will be sweet.

Scripture Reading
Psalm 119:165, The Message
Proverbs 3:24, NIV

Day 15

MORNING

The Lord Almighty declared that in this place He would give peace. We receive this promise for our household and our future generations.

EVENING

I pray for the Lord to keep you safe even when you are alone. You will lie down in peace and sleep.

Scripture Reading
Haggai 2:9, NIV
Psalm 4:8, TLB

Day 16

MORNING

I pray that you will hear, understand and trust the words of Jesus; then you will be unshakable and assured, deeply at peace. Even though you will experience difficulties in this godless world, you will take heart because Jesus conquered the world!

EVENING

God has provided for your wholeness. Since you have been made right in His sight by faith in His promises, you can have real peace because of what Jesus Christ our Lord has done for you.

Scripture Reading
John 16:33
Romans 5:2

Day 17

MORNING

I approach His throne of grace with you, our baby, thanking Him for a peaceful day because Christ Himself is our way of peace.

EVENING

May you experience His peace, which is far more wonderful than the human mind can understand. His peace will keep your thoughts and heart quiet and at rest as we trust in Christ Jesus.

Scripture Reading
Ephesians 2:14, TLB
Philippians 4:7

Day 18

MORNING

As I train you up, my child, I purpose to let the peace (soul harmony which comes) from the Christ rule (act as umpire continually) in my heart—deciding and settling with finality all questions that arise in my mind.

EVENING

May I be a blessing to you, and teach you how to get along with others. I ask God to give you His wisdom that is gentle and reasonable, overflowing with mercy and blessings, not hot one day and cold the next, not two-faced. May He create in you a desire to be like Jesus.

Scripture Reading
Colossians 3:15, AMP
James 3:17, THE MESSAGE

Day 19

MORNING

May you run away from infantile indulgence as you develop spiritually, mentally, emotionally and physically. I believe that you will run after mature righteousness—faith, love and peace—joining those who are in honest and serious prayer before God.

EVENING

I pray that you will stay close to anything that makes you want to do right. You will have faith and love, and you will enjoy the companionship of those who love the Lord and have pure hearts.

Note to parents: Praying for and speaking blessings at the family altar over your child's future will plant seeds in his or her spiritual mind and prepare him or her to receive godly instruction. Your prayers and words of blessing will allow our Gardener, God, to landscape him or her with the Word, making a salvation-garden of your child's life.

Scripture Reading
2 Timothy 2:22, The Message, TLB

Day 20

MORNING

I purpose to bless you with peacemaking techniques through instruction and practice. You will be blessed when you can show people how to cooperate instead of compete or fight. That's when you will discover who you really are and find your place in God's family.

EVENING

I thank the God of love and peace for bringing you into completeness of personality. You will be of good comfort, be of one mind and live in peace.

Scripture Reading
Matthew 5:9, The Message
2 Corinthians 13:11, NKJV

Day 21

MORNING

If it is possible, as far as it depends on you, may you live at peace with everyone.

EVENING

God will establish peace for you, ______, for you have come from Him.

Scripture Reading
Romans 12:18, NIV
Isaiah 26:12, NIV, TLB

MORNING

I pray that you will be a blameless man (or woman) and walk uprightly, for your future will be one of peace.

EVENING

I pray for the Lord to help me remember and teach you to stir up goodness, peace and joy from the Holy Spirit. May you pursue the things that make for peace and the things by which one may edify another.

Scripture Reading
Psalm 37:37, NKJV
Romans 4:17–19, NKJV, TLB

Day 23

MORNING

I thank the Father for blessing you. You will live in joy and peace. The mountains and hills, the trees of the field—all the world around you—will rejoice.

EVENING

I thank the Lord of peace for being with you as you sleep. Now may the Lord of peace Himself give you peace at all times and in every way. May the Lord be with you.

Scripture Reading
Isaiah 55:12, TLB
2 Thessalonians 3:16, NIV

Day 24

MORNING

May the God of hope fill you, ______, with all joy and peace in believing so that you may abound in hope by the power of the Holy Spirit.

EVENING

He sent His Holy Spirit to teach you, ______, and to lead you into all truth. I pray that you shall be taught by the Lord. Great shall be your peace.

Scripture Reading
Romans 15:13, NKJV
John 16:13, The Message
Isaiah 54:13, NKJV

Day 25

MORNING

I pray that you will grow in spiritual strength and become more intimately acquainted with our Lord and Savior Jesus Christ. To Him be all glory and splendid honor, both now and forevermore.

EVENING

The Holy Spirit, who is Truth, has come. I thank Him for guiding you into all Truth. He will be passing on to you what He has heard. He will tell you about the future.

Scripture Reading
2 Peter 3:18, TLB
John 16:13, TLB

Day 26

MORNING

I purpose to be a constant example to you in helping the poor. I remember the words of the Lord Jesus, "It is more blessed to give than to receive."

EVENING

In stressful moments, may the Holy Spirit remind you of the words of our Lord, "It's all right. Don't be afraid!"

Scripture Reading
Acts 20:35, TLB
Judges 6:23, TLB

Day 27

MORNING

God knows the refinement that you will need. I pray that you will submit to the constant ministry of transformation by the Holy Spirit. You will learn right from wrong as you practice doing right.

EVENING

Nothing will please me more than to find you walking in Truth, just as I have been commanded by Him to do.

Scripture Reading
2 Corinthians 3:18, AMP
Hebrews 5:14, TLB
2 John 4, AMP

Day 28

MORNING

I pray that you will not copy the behavior and customs of this world, but be a new and different person with a fresh newness in all you do and think. Then you will learn from your own experience how His ways will really satisfy you.

EVENING

I pray and believe that you will turn your back on sin and do good. You will embrace peace—you will not let it get away!

Scripture Reading
Romans 12:2, TLB
Psalm 34:14–15, THE MESSAGE

MORNING

I bless you with His love and wisdom. I believe that you will be very careful in how you live—making the most of every opportunity you have for doing good.

EVENING

In the name of Jesus, I bind your plans for the future to His plans for you. May God give you a clear vision for the future. The vision is yet for an appointed time . . . though it tarry, you will wait for it because it will surely come.

Scripture Reading
Ephesians 5:15–16, NIV, TLB
Matthew 18:18
Habakkuk 2:3, KJV

Day 30

MORNING

The Holy Spirit is your Strengthener and Standby. I pray that you won't get tired of doing what is right, for after a while you will reap a harvest of blessing if you don't get discouraged and give up. The vision will come to pass.

EVENING

I pray and believe that as the deer pants for streams of water, so shall your soul pant for God. I pray that your soul will thirst for the living God. I ask the Holy Spirit to show you where to go and meet with God.

Scripture Reading
Galatians 6:9, TLB
Psalm 42:1–2, NIV

Day 31

MORNING

I pray and believe that you will humble yourself before God, and you shall be given every blessing and shall have wonderful peace.

EVENING

I pray that you will walk blamelessly before God. A wonderful future lies ahead for the good, blameless, upright man or woman. There is a happy ending for you.

Scripture Reading

Psalm 37:11, TLB
Deuteronomy 18:13, TLB
Psalm 37:37, TLB

AUGUST

Learn to Listen and Pray

August

PRAY, LISTEN AND REST

In the still moments of the morning and evening, hold your young child in your arms, pray and listen. What is the Lord saying to you today? Is He revealing His plans for you and your child? Do you sense His presence in the stillness?

As you thank the Lord, praise Him, bless Him and speak blessings over your child each morning and night, don't forget to also spend quiet time with Him. It is often in those moments that He will reveal Himself to you in deeper and broader ways. He may also surprise you with instruction and guidance on situations that seemed to be impossible just moments ago. "Call to me and I will answer you and tell you great and unsearchable things you do not know" (Jer. 33:3, NIV).

If we do not purpose to set aside quiet time with the Lord, it is easy to get caught up in the hustle and bustle and duties of life. Oftentimes, we then begin to work in our own strength because we have not been relying on Him for His strength. Then we often become consumed with worries and distracted by the natural world. If we disregard our spiritual needs, His voice will be further and further drowned out by the cares of this life. Bit by bit our peace can be replaced by confusion, a short temper, feelings of being overwhelmed and exhaustion.

It may seem that having a young child in the house makes it impossible to spend time with the Lord, but moving from duty to duty without spending any quiet time with the Lord will only make matters worse. You were called to peace, not constant hardship. Yes, there is labor and trouble in this life, but Jesus sent the Holy Spirit to comfort and to guide you. Do not let the workload or problems of the day rule your day; instead, look for moments to rest in Him. "Let the peace of Christ rule in your hearts, since as members of one body you were called to peace. And be thankful" (Col. 3:15, NIV).

Jesus wants to give you rest. He wants you to lay your burdens at His feet and rest from your own labors. Many times we just make life too hard. If we would only be transparent and take our burdens to the Lord, our loads would be so much lighter. Jesus said, "Come to me, all you who are weary and burdened, and I will give you rest. Take my yoke upon you and learn from me, for I am gentle and humble in heart, and you will find rest for your souls. For my yoke is easy and my burden is light" (Matt. 11:28–30, NIV).

There is a place of rest that we obtain when we lay our burdens at His feet and our concerns in His hands. We can also rest in the fact that we have a High Priest who understands our weaknesses. He is ready to help us. He knows the temptations and struggles we face. In Him, we will find the help we need. We may think we know what we need, but time and again we discover that His thoughts and ways are above our own. His answer is always exactly what we needed. "Let us then approach the throne of grace with confidence, so that we may receive mercy and find grace to help us in our time of need" (Heb. 4:16, NIV).

We can rest in the fact that we are heavenly bound. He is working in us and through us. "Lord, you establish peace for us; all that we have accomplished you have done for us" (Isa. 26:12, NIV).

Day 1

MORNING

______, you will learn to listen with expectancy to what God will say. He speaks peace to His people. God shall make His footsteps a way in which you are to follow.

EVENING

______, I bless you and pray that you will fully obey the Lord your God and carefully follow all His commandments. The Lord your God will set you high above all the nations on earth.

Scripture Reading
Psalm 85:8, 13, AMP
Deuteronomy 28:1, NIV

Day 2

MORNING

______, you are learning to listen to the voice of the Lord your God. He will bring you peace. When God speaks to you say, "Speak, Lord, for your servant is listening."

EVENING

This evening, our little one, we receive the good gifts of the Father above. We ask Him for comfort and peace, believing in our heavenly Father's goodness.

Scripture Reading
1 Samuel 3:9, NIV
Matthew 7:11, NIV

Day 3

MORNING

God has redeemed us. Greater is He that is in us than he that is in the world.

EVENING

This evening I thank God for His Word that will sustain us. He will never allow the (consistently) righteous to be moved (made to slip, fall, or fail.) Our little child, the Lord cares for you affectionately and cares about you watchfully.

Scripture Reading
Psalm 55:1, NIV
1 John 4:4, NIV
Psalm 55:22, AMP
1 Peter 5:7, AMP

Day 4

MORNING

______, I bless you and pray that you will always listen to the Lord. You will be blessed when you listen to the voice of the Good Shepherd. I pledge myself to help you watch daily at His doors and to wait at His doorway. You will find life and receive favor from the Lord.

EVENING

Baby ______, together we will learn psalms and hymns, sing spiritual songs and make melody in our hearts to the Lord. Give thanks always for all things unto God and the Father in the name of our Lord Jesus Christ.

Scripture Reading
Proverbs 8:34–35, NIV
Ephesians 5:19–20, KJV

Day 5

MORNING

______, I pray that you will always obey God. May you walk in all the ways He has commanded you so that it may go well with you. I believe that you will grow up listening to God.

EVENING

I thank the Father for the good work He has begun in you. I am confident that He will carry it on to completion until the day of Christ Jesus.

Scripture Reading
Jeremiah 7:23; 11:4, NIV
Philippians 1:4–7, NIV

Day 6

MORNING

Now I pray that our God will hear the prayers and petitions of His servants. I pause and listen for His Spirit. May His peace surround us. I thank God that you, ______, are learning to listen to God.

EVENING

This evening I will not fret or worry about you and your future, but in everything by prayer and supplication with thanksgiving, I will make my requests known to God.

Scripture Reading
Daniel 9:17, NIV
Philippians 4:6–7, KJV

Day 7

MORNING

______, you are my son (or daughter), whom I love; with you I am well pleased.

EVENING

Beloved child of the Lord, I give thanks always to God for you, because God chose you from the beginning for salvation. You were chosen out of the world, and you are a special child to God and to me.

Scripture Reading
Matthew 17:5, NIV
2 Thessalonians 2:13, AMP
John 15:19

Day 8

MORNING

Jesus made it possible for us to have access by one Spirit unto the heavenly Father. In Him, we have boldness and access with confidence by faith. By faith, you shall stand firm.

EVENING

For the Lord shall be your confidence, firm and strong; He shall keep your foot from being caught in a trap or some hidden danger. Listen to the words of peace from the Lord.

Scripture Reading
Ephesians 2:18; 3:12, KJV
2 Corinthians 1:24
Proverbs 3:26, AMP

MORNING

Listen to the Lord, ______, for He stands at the door and knocks. If you hear His voice and open the door, He will come in and eat with you, and you with Him. Are you awake? Listen and enjoy the company of the Lord.

EVENING

______, I praise our Lord tonight. He promised that when we are speaking and praying, making our requests to Him, He will come to give us insight and understanding. He is to be highly esteemed.

Scripture Reading

Revelation 3:20, NIV, THE MESSAGE
Daniel 9:20–23, NIV

Day 10

MORNING

______, at all times you can call upon the name of the Lord our God, and He will be right there to keep you safe.

EVENING

May God anoint your ears to always listen to the Lord, for He will never forsake you. Your inheritance is that His good Spirit will instruct you.

Scripture Reading
1 Samuel 7:5–8, NIV
1 Samuel 17:47, NIV
Nehemiah 9:20, AMP

Day 11

MORNING

May you be content today and at peace. May you acquire the life skills that will make you a whole person, complete in Jesus.

EVENING

You, ______, will abide in God's presence, and His Holy Spirit shall be with you and in you. The word is near you; it is in your mouth and in your heart.

Scripture Reading
2 Samuel 7:27, NIV
Psalm 51:11, AMP
Romans 10:8, NIV

Day 12

MORNING

I ask the Lord our God to give attention to His servant's prayer and plea for mercy. I thank Him for leading you into that land flowing with milk and honey, that your life may be sweet and prosperous.

EVENING

Praised (honored, blessed) be the God and Father of our Lord Jesus Christ (the Messiah)! You, our little baby, have been born to receive an ever-living hope through the resurrection of Jesus. You are born into an inheritance that is beyond the reach of destruction.

Scripture Reading

1 Kings 8:28, NIV
Numbers 14:8
1 Peter 1:3–4, AMP

Day 13

MORNING

May the Lord guide you and reveal His will to you. You will pray to Him, and He will hear you, and you will fulfill your vows. What you decide on will be done, and light will shine on your ways.

EVENING

I ask God to wake you, our baby, each morning with the sound of His loving voice. You are learning to go to sleep each night trusting in Him. I ask the Lord to point out the road you must travel; you are all ears, and your eyes are before Him.

Scripture Reading
Job 22:27–28, NIV
Psalm 143:9–10, The Message

Day 14

MORNING

I purpose to teach you, my child, to come to Him in prayer. As your prayer comes before the Lord, I ask Him to turn His ear to your cry. You will prosper and grow in wisdom and in understanding.

EVENING

I bless you, my child, that you might take a firm stand and a tight grip on what you are taught about God. May Jesus Himself and God our Father, who reached out in love, invigorate you and enliven you.

Scripture Reading
Psalm 65:2, NIV
Psalm 88:2, NIV
2 Thessalonians 2:15–17, The Message

Day 15

MORNING

Good morning, ______. God calls you righteous. The prayer of the upright pleases Him. Listen, and God will bring you peace.

EVENING

Listen, baby ______, and hear what Jesus said. He says that if you believe in Him, the works that He does, you will do even greater. You have a wonderful future prepared for you.

Scripture Reading
Proverbs 15:8, 29, NIV
John 14:11–12, KJV

Day 16

MORNING

______, whatever you ask for according to the will of God, believe that you have received it, and it will be yours. Thank you for listening to the Lord.

EVENING

Surely God is your salvation. You will trust and not be afraid. The Lord is your strength and song.

Scripture Reading
Mark 11:24, NIV
Isaiah 12:2, NIV

Day 17

MORNING

Baby ______, as you grow up, devote yourself to prayer, being watchful and thankful. Let the peace of Christ rule in your heart, for you are a member of one body, which is called to peace.

EVENING

______, our Father wants to hear your voice, for your voice is sweet and your face lovely.

Scripture Reading
Colossians 4:2, NIV
Colossians 3:15, NIV
Song of Solomon 2:14, NIV

Day 18

MORNING

This morning I call to God, knowing that He will answer us. He will show us great and mighty things, which we do not know. How I love to listen to our God.

EVENING

______, be still and wait for the Lord God, and you will be glad and rejoice in His salvation.

Scripture Reading
Jeremiah 33:3, NKJV
Isaiah 25:9, NKJV

Day 19

MORNING

Today, ______, I will pray to our heavenly Father in the name of Jesus and not lose heart. Listen to the Lord and be encouraged.

EVENING

This evening I know that God is spirit, and His worshipers must worship in spirit and in truth. Be blessed with the knowledge, ______, that Messiah has come, and He will come again.

Scripture Reading
Luke 18:1, 8, NKJV
John 4:24–26, NIV

Day 20

MORNING

Sweet one, we will go into your room and pray to our Father who is in the secret place; your Father who sees in secret will reward you.

EVENING

This evening, I give thanks to God the Father of our Lord Jesus Christ, praying always for you. You shall bring forth good fruit and know the grace of God in truth and love in the Spirit.

Scripture Reading
Matthew 6:6, NKJV
Colossians 1:1–8, KJV

Day 21

MORNING

This day may you, _____, be strengthened with all might, according to God's glorious power, unto all patience and longsuffering with joyfulness. I give thanks to our heavenly Father and come near to call upon Him in truth. He will fulfill the desire of those who fear Him; He also will hear their cry and save them.

EVENING

_____, since the day I knew you were on the way, I have not ceased to give thanks for you. I desire that you might be filled with the knowledge of God's will in all wisdom and spiritual understanding.

Scripture Reading
Psalm 145:18–19, NKJV
Colossians 1:9–13, KJV

Day 22

MORNING

______, I pray that you will listen to what the Lord will say. When you delight yourself in the Lord, He will give you the desires of your heart.

EVENING

Baby ______, I bless you and pray for you continually. I will watch over you with prayer and thanksgiving. Even as I teach you of the mystery of Christ, I will continue in prayer for you. I will labor fervently for you in prayers, that you may stand perfect and complete in all the will of God.

Scripture Reading
Psalm 85:8, NIV
Psalm 37:4, NKJV
Colossians 4:2–4, 12, 17

Day 23

MORNING

______, the Lord hears the prayer of the righteous. Listen to the Holy Spirit as He teaches you obedience.

EVENING

Little one, I desire to be an example to you and to pray always without ceasing. When you are older you will pray and give thanks in everything, for this is the will of God in Christ Jesus concerning you, ______.

Scripture Reading
Proverbs 15:29, NKJV
1 Thessalonians 5:17–18, KJV

Day 24

MORNING

Baby ______, Jesus is our Great High Priest, and He gives us ready access to God—so let's not let it slip through our fingers. Let's come boldly to the throne of grace and ask Him for what is so readily available for us. We will receive God's mercy and accept His help.

EVENING

Thanks be to God for you, baby ______, beloved of the Lord. From the beginning God chose you to salvation through sanctification of the Spirit and belief of the truth. God loves you and has given you everlasting consolation and good hope through grace.

Scripture Reading
Hebrews 4:14–16, KJV, THE MESSAGE
2 Thessalonians 2:13, 16–17

Day 25

MORNING

Today, I shall pray to God for you, ______, and He will delight in you. The Lord our God is in our midst; the Mighty One saves. He rejoices over you with gladness. He quiets you with His love, and He rejoices over you with singing.

EVENING

______, let us praise God for the creation He has made. In the beginning, He laid the foundation of the earth, and the heavens are the works of His hands.

Scripture Reading
Zephaniah 3:17, NKJV
Hebrews 1:10–12, KJV

Day 26

MORNING

This morning, I pray to the Lord for He is good, and He gives abundant mercy to all those who call upon Him. When we call Him, He will answer.

EVENING

Baby, we will watch in hope for the Lord. Let's wait for God our Savior; He will hear us. Learn to listen to God, for He brings us peace.

Scripture Reading
Psalm 86:5, 7, NKJV
Micah 7:7, NIV

Day 27

MORNING

______, this morning I draw near to minister to our God. When we pray and draw near to God, He will draw near to us. Always put your trust in Him and listen to His voice.

EVENING

______, there will be times when you lack wisdom. Ask God, and He will liberally give His wisdom to you so that you will know what to do. Do not waiver, but ask in faith. Every good and perfect gift is from above and comes down from the Father of lights, with whom is no variableness, neither shadow of turning.

Scripture Reading
James 4:8, NKJV
James 1:5–8, 17, KJV

Day 28

MORNING

At evening, at morning and at noon, ______, we will pray, and our heavenly Father shall hear our voice. You will learn to make your requests known to your heavenly Father, for He loves and cares for you. You are at peace because we have a loving God.

EVENING

______, if you are ever in trouble, you should pray. If you are happy, sing songs of praise. Little one, I entreat you to listen to God, for He will give you His peace.

Scripture Reading
Psalm 55:17, NKJV
James 5:13–18, NIV

Day 29

MORNING

______, as you mature, you will learn that all the ways of the Lord are loving and faithful. You please God when you believe that He is real and that He rewards those who truly want to find Him.

EVENING

Our little baby, what a God we have! The Father of Jesus has given us a brand-new life so that we have everything to live for, including a future in heaven, which starts now. God is keeping careful watch over you. The day is coming when you will have it all.

Scripture Reading
Psalm 25:9, NIV
Hebrews 11:6, NCV
1 Peter 1:3–4, The Message

Day 30

MORNING

______, the Holy Spirit will teach you to pray, and you shall pray without ceasing. He will give you a grateful heart, and you will give thanks. Pray and listen to your God.

EVENING

______, the God of all grace, who has called us into His eternal glory by Christ Jesus, will make you perfect, establish, strengthen and settle you. To God be glory and dominion forever and ever. Amen.

Scripture Reading
1 Thessalonians 5:17–18, NKJV
1 Peter 5:10–11, NKJV

Day 31

MORNING

Our little one, you are wise, and shine like the brightness of the firmament. You will turn many to righteousness, and like the stars they will be too numerous to count. Persist in listening to God.

EVENING

As you learn and grow, little one, I bless you with God's Word, which says that if you call to Him, He will answer you and tell you great and unsearchable things you do not know.

Scripture Reading
Daniel 12:3, NIV
Jeremiah 33:3, NIV

SEPTEMBER

The Good Shepherd Carries His Lambs

HIS BLESSINGS

No book written by man could possibly number the blessings of God or measure His goodness. Yes, we can learn of Him in many ways, but who can even begin to comprehend the goodness of God? Each day can be a new discovery of learning more about Him. Our revelation of His character can be increased each day. In fact, we are to receive the fresh manna, the fresh bread, of the Word of God each day.

In Psalm 119:105 we are told that God's Word will light the path we are to follow: "Thy word is a lamp unto my feet, and a light unto my path" (KJV). As you speak these blessings over your child and read the recommended scriptures, you will learn and be reminded of the abundance of God's goodness, mercy and blessings. It is my prayer that your understanding of His power and your knowledge of Him will increase with each passing day and that you will pass the truth of God's Word on to your children and your children's children.

Just how expansive are the blessings that the Lord has stored up for you and your child? The answer is simple: Every good thing is available to you in Christ Jesus if you walk uprightly before Him. "The LORD God is a sun and shield: the LORD will give grace and glory: no good thing will he withhold from them that walk uprightly" (Ps. 84:11, KJV).

Through knowledge of Him, you will be given everything you need—not just some of the things you need, but all. By His power, He is able and He wants to provide for all your spiritual and physical needs. "His divine power has given us everything we need for life and godliness through our knowledge of him who called us by his own glory and goodness" (2 Pet. 1:3, NIV).

Even when situations look impossible, He is more than able to provide for you. He will make it possible for you to be successful as a parent and in every other good thing you do. "And God is able to make all grace abound to you, so that in all things at all times, having all that you need, you will abound in every good work. As it is written: 'He has scattered abroad his gifts to the poor; his righteousness endures forever'" (2 Cor. 9:8–9, NIV). In Him lies all wisdom, and by the grace of God in Christ Jesus, you have access to that wisdom. Go boldly before Him in faith and ask Him for His wisdom. He is your help in time of need. His answers may not always come in ways we expect, but His ways are always perfect.

As you bless your child each day, remember that God is a rewarder of them who diligently seek Him. You and your child are part of the family of God and are therefore inheritors of all things in Christ Jesus. You are partakers of an inheritance that will never fade away. Old things become new in Christ Jesus, the Author and the Finisher of our faith. "In his great mercy he has given us new birth into a living hope through the resurrection of Jesus Christ from the dead, and into an inheritance that can never perish, spoil or fade—kept in heaven for you, who through faith are shielded by God's power until the coming of the salvation that is ready to be revealed in the last time" (1 Pet. 1:3–5, NIV)

When you go with your child before the Father in a

time of a need, you can go boldly before the throne of grace, knowing that He will answer and that His Word will come to pass. He is ready to commune with you and to work on your behalf. He is ready to save, to heal and deliver. "Unto you that fear my name shall the Sun of righteousness arise with healing in his wing" (Mal. 4:2, KJV).

Day 1

MORNING

I pray that you, my little one, will know this: God is God, and God, God. He made you; we didn't make God. We're His people, ______, and you are His well-tended sheep.

EVENING

______, Jesus is the Good Shepherd, and He tends His flock well. He gathers the lambs in His arms and carries them close to His heart. He will gently lead you, my little one.

Scripture Reading
Psalm 100:3, THE MESSAGE
Isaiah 40:11, NIV

Day 2

MORNING

I pray and believe that you will love Jesus, and that you will feed His sheep.

EVENING

I pray that you will put God in charge of your work so that what you have planned will take place.

Scripture Reading
John 21:15
Proverbs 16:3, The Message

Day 3

MORNING

I confirm that the Lord will fulfill His promise to make our sons flourish in their youth like well-nurtured plants, and our daughters to be like graceful pillars, carved to beautify a palace.

EVENING

His blessings shall come upon you and overtake you if you heed His voice. You will come short in no gift.

Scripture Reading
Psalm 144:12, NLT
Deuteronomy 28:2
1 Corinthians 1:7, NKJV

Day 4

MORNING

______, God has given each of us the ability to do certain things well. Therefore, if God has given you the ability to prophesy, then I bless you to prophesy whenever you can—as often as your faith is strong enough to receive a message from God.

EVENING

______, if your gift is that of serving others, may you serve them well. If you are a teacher, I believe that you will do a good job of teaching. If you are a preacher, may God see to it that your sermons are strong and helpful.

Scripture Reading
Romans 12:6–7, TLB

Day 5

MORNING

______, I continue to pray for your divine destiny. If God gives you money, I pray that you will be generous in helping others with it. If God gives you ability and puts you in charge of the work of others, I pray that you will take the responsibility seriously. I believe that you will always offer comfort and Christian cheer to the sorrowful.

EVENING

______,I confess that the Lord is your Shepherd and you will have everything you need! As you sleep tonight, God will let you rest in the meadow grass and lead you beside the quiet streams. He will give you new strength and help you do what honors Him most.

Scripture Reading
Romans 12:7–8, TLB
Psalm 23:1–2, TLB

Day 6

MORNING

Because the Lord is your Shepherd, He will feed, guide and shield you. You shall not lack. Even when the way goes through Death Valley, you will not be afraid. When you walk at His side, His trusty shepherd's crook makes you feel secure.

EVENING

I acknowledge the Lord as your Shepherd. His rod (to protect) and His staff (to guide) will comfort you. He prepares a table before you in the presence of your enemies. He anoints you with oil; your (brimming) cup will run over.

Scripture Reading
Psalm 23, AMP, THE MESSAGE

Day 7

MORNING

______, I pray and believe that only goodness, mercy and unfailing love shall follow you all the days of your life. Through the length of days the house of the Lord (and His presence) shall be your dwelling place.

EVENING

______, I thank the Lord for showing you the path where you should go, for pointing out the right road for you to walk. He will lead you and teach you, for He is the God who gives you salvation. Our hope is in Him.

Scripture Reading
Psalm 23:6, AMP
Psalm 25:4–5, TLB

Day 8

MORNING

______, I lay hands on you and dedicate you to the Lord. I pray that you will teach others to observe everything that He will command you, and that He will be with you all the days, perpetually, uniformly and on every occasion—to the [very] close and consummation of the age.

EVENING

Little one, I bless you and pray that you will keep your eyes on Jesus, who both began and finished this race you're in. I pray for our heavenly Father to give you the desire to study how Jesus did it and to give you the courage to fulfill your destiny.

Scripture Reading
Matthew 28:20, AMP
Hebrews 12:2, THE MESSAGE

Day 9

MORNING

I pray that you will wash your hands in innocence so you may go about His altar. May you publish with the voice of thanksgiving and tell of all His wondrous works.

EVENING

I ask the Holy Spirit to teach you to trust God from the bottom of your heart. Then you will not try to figure out everything on your own.

Scripture Reading
Psalm 26:6–7, KJV, NKJV
Proverbs 3:5, THE MESSAGE

Day 10

MORNING

I thank God for being your hiding place from every storm of life; He even will keep you from getting into trouble! He surrounds you with songs of victory.

EVENING

God is a safe place for you to hide, and He is ready to help when you need Him. You can stand fearless at the cliff-edge of doom and courageous in a sea storm and earthquake, before the rush and roar of oceans or in the tremors that shift mountains. I thank God for fighting for you and surrounding you with armies of angels to protect you.

Scripture Reading
Psalm 37:7, TLB
Psalm 46:1–3, The Message

Day 11

MORNING

May you be steadfast and immovable, always abounding in the work of the Lord.

EVENING

I thank Father God for the Holy Spirit, who helps me intercede for you. I know that all things will work together for your good because I am praying for Him to give you a heart to love Him. He has called you according to His purpose and predestined you to be conformed to the image of His Son.

Scripture Reading
1 Corinthians 15:58, NAS
Romans 8:26–29, NKJV

Day 12

MORNING

I commit you, ______, into our Father's keeping. I know the One in whom I trust, and I am sure that He is able to safely guard all that I have given Him until the day of Christ's return.

EVENING

I ask the Holy Spirit to help me to teach you, my child, to pray at all times. May you ask God for anything in line with the Holy Spirit's wishes. You will learn how to plead with God and to keep praying earnestly for all Christians everywhere.

Scripture Reading
2 Timothy 1:12
Ephesians 6:18, TLB

Day 13

MORNING

I pray that others can see that you, ______, are a letter from Christ, written by me. It is not a letter written with pen and ink, but by the Spirit of the living God; not one carved on stone, but in human hearts.

EVENING

May the God, who has shepherded me all of my life, wonderfully bless you, my child.

Scripture Reading
2 Corinthians 3:3, TLB
Genesis 48:15, TLB

Day 14

MORNING

I thank God for protecting you. He will defend you, for He defends and blesses His chosen ones. He will lead you like a shepherd and carry you forever in His arms.

EVENING

May the Shepherd of Israel, who leads Israel like a flock, lead you, our little one. I pray for God, who is enthroned above the guardian angels, to bend down His ear and listen as I plead for Him to display His power and radiant glory to you.

Scripture Reading
Psalm 28:8–9, TLB
Psalm 80:1, TLB

Day 15

MORNING

______, I believe that you are good ground. I pray for God to plant His Word deep in your heart that you might not sin against Him.

EVENING

He will shepherd you with His staff, for you are a member of the flock of His inheritance.

Scripture Reading
Mark 4:20, NKJV
Psalm 119:11
Micah 7:14, NIV

MORNING

I pray that you will think much about His words and store them in your heart so that they will hold you back from sin.

EVENING

Jesus is the Good Shepherd. ______, you have been born for His glory. He knows His own sheep, and you will know His voice, for you are one of His.

Scripture Reading
Psalm 119:11, TLB
John 10:14, THE MESSAGE

Day 17

MORNING

This is the day our Lord has made. I ask the God of peace, who brought again from the dead our Lord Jesus, to equip you with all you need for doing His will.

EVENING

May the God of peace put you together, provide you with everything you need to please Him and make you into what gives Him most pleasure, by means of the sacrifice of Jesus, the Messiah. All glory to Jesus forever and always! Amen!

Scripture Reading
Hebrews 13:20–21, The Message, tlb

Day 18

MORNING

I bless you, my son (or daughter), to come, listen and let me teach you the importance of fearing the Lord. The fear of the Lord is the beginning of wisdom.

EVENING

I submit to the Lamb on the throne who will shepherd you and lead you to spring waters of life.

Scripture Reading
Psalm 34:11, TLB
Revelation 7:17

Day 19

MORNING

It comforts me to know that Jehovah God spreads His wings over you, even as an eagle overspreads her young. The eagle carries them upon her wings—as does the Lord carry His people!

EVENING

May you run the race that is before you and never give up.

Scripture Reading
Deuteronomy 32:9–11, TLB
Hebrews 12:1, NCV

Day 20

MORNING

Good morning! I acknowledge that our Father is this great God, and He is our God forever and ever. He will be your guide until you complete your life here on earth.

EVENING

God has given you some special abilities. With His help, I will encourage you to use them to help others, passing on to others God's many blessings.

Scripture Reading
Psalm 48:14, TLB
1 Peter 4:10, TLB

Day 21

MORNING

I pray and believe that you will be generous with the different things God has given you. You will pass them around to all. If words, let it be God's words; if help, let it be God's hearty help.

EVENING

You shall be like a tree planted by the rivers of water, that brings forth its fruit in its season, whose leaf shall not wither. Whatever you do shall prosper.

Scripture Reading
1 Peter 4:10, THE MESSAGE
Psalm 1:4, NKJV

Day 22

MORNING

I ask our heavenly Father to give me wisdom to monitor what you hear and see. I believe that you will grow up to be a godly man (or woman), and out of the good treasure of your heart you will bring forth good. Out of the abundance of the heart your mouth will speak.

EVENING

The Lord answered my request and gave me a child. Our heart rejoices in the Lord; our horn is exalted in the Lord; I smile at our enemies because I rejoice in His salvation.

Scripture Reading
Luke 6:43–45, NKJV
1 Samuel 2:1

Day 23

MORNING

Little one, I pray that you will hear instruction and be wise, and not disdain it.

EVENING

I bless you and ask the Holy Spirit to counsel you, give you wisdom in the night and tell you what to do. May you always think of the Lord; because He is so near, you will never need to stumble or fall.

Scripture Reading
Proverbs 8:33, NKJV
Psalm 16:7, TLB

Day 24

MORNING

I thank the Sovereign Lord for helping you, _____. When you are older, you will set your face like a flint and do right things. I know you will not be put to shame.

EVENING

I pray that you will store up for yourself treasures in heaven, where moth and rust do not destroy and where thieves do not break in and steal. For where your treasure is, there your heart will be also.

Scripture Reading
Isaiah 50:7, NIV
Matthew 6:20–21, NIV

Day 25

MORNING

Little one, I pray that when the time comes for you to decide whom you will obey, you will have the courage to say, "But as for me and my family, we will serve the Lord."

EVENING

I pray that you will call to the Lord, and He will answer you and tell you great and mighty things, fenced in and hidden, which you do not know or understand.

Scripture Reading
Joshua 24:15, TLB
Jeremiah 33:3, AMP

Day 26

MORNING

______, here we are on this glorious morning in the presence of God to thank Him for this day He has made. I am confident that when you seek Him, you will find Him. You will call upon Him while He is near.

EVENING

May you know joy by the answer of the Holy Spirit's mouth; a word spoken in due season, how good it is!

Scripture Reading
Isaiah 55:6, TLB
Proverbs 15:23, NKJV

Day 27

MORNING

Litle one, I bless you this morning. May the Lord guide you continually, satisfy you with all good things and keep you healthy, too. Then you will be like a well-watered garden, like an ever-flowing spring.

EVENING

______, I ask the Lord to teach us to pray. I thank Him for His angels that encamp round about us to keep us safe throughout the night.

Scripture Reading
Isaiah 58:11, TLB
Luke 11:1

Day 28

MORNING

______, you belong to God. When you pass through the deep waters, He will be with you; your troubles will not overwhelm you.

EVENING

______, when you are faced with obstacles, may the Holy Spirit remind you of God's Word that says, "I can do all things through Christ who strengthens me."

Scripture Reading
Isaiah 43:1–2, TEV
Philippians 4:13, NKJV

Day 29

MORNING

Each morning I look to our Father in heaven and lay our requests before Him, praying earnestly. This is the confidence that we have in Him, that if we ask anything according to His will, He will hear us.

EVENING

I ask the Lord to give me the wisdom to teach you, ______, to wait upon Him. When you wait upon the Lord, He shall renew your strength. You shall mount up with wings like eagles; you shall run and not be weary; you shall walk and not faint.

Scripture Reading
Psalm 5:3, TLB
1 John 5:14
Isaiah 40:31, TLB

Day 30

MORNING

______, this is the day that the Lord has made. I come with you, our baby, before the Lord rejoicing, and we will be glad throughout the day. He has given us a joyous spirit and a glad heart.

EVENING

May you delight yourself in the Lord, and He will cause you to ride on the high hills of the earth.

Scripture Reading
Psalm 118:24
Isaiah 58:14, NKJV

OCTOBER

Be Not Afraid

HIS WORD WILL COME TO PASS

The Word of the Lord will endure forever. It will not change. You can count on it. You can fully put your trust in His Truth. "But the word of the Lord stands forever" (1 Pet. 1:25, NIV). Because the blessings contained in this book are taken from the Word of God, you can be sure that your words will not fail. A great harvest of fruit will be produced by your words of blessing.

The Bible is not mere words of men. The Scriptures were fully inspired by God. The Word of God testifies of this very fact. Because the Scriptures are from God, they are fully reliable, infallible and trustworthy. "All scripture is given by inspiration of God" (2 Tim. 3:16, KJV). "For the prophecy came not in old time by the will of man: but holy men of God spake as they were moved by the Holy Ghost" (2 Pet. 1:21, KJV).

The Bible tells us that Jesus Christ is the Word of God that was made flesh. Therefore, putting your trust in Jesus Christ is also putting your trust in the Word of God. "And the Word was made flesh, and dwelt among us, (and we beheld his glory, the glory as of the only begotten of the Father,) full of grace and truth" (John 1:14, KJV).

Jesus Christ loved us so much that He gave Himself for us as an offering for our sins. Because of this, we are saved, healed and delivered. God speaks His truth to us through His Son, Jesus Christ, the Word of God revealed in the flesh. "God, who at sundry times and in divers manners spake in time past unto the fathers by the prophets, hath in these last days spoken unto us by his Son, whom he hath appointed heir of all things, by whom also he made the worlds" (Heb. 1:1, KJV).

God is love, and the Word of God is the revelation of that love. His love and His Word will never fail. It will come to pass. Yes, we must obey Him and do our part, but we have the assurance that our steps will be ordered by Him if we follow His Word and His ways. When we accept Jesus as our Lord and Savior and serve Him and Him only, He is our beginning, our end and everything in between.

God's Word will accomplish what He sent it forth to do in your life and in the life of your child. His purpose for which He sent it forth to do in your lives will surely come to pass. "As the rain and the snow come down from heaven, and do not return to it without watering the earth and making it bud and flourish, so that it yields seed for the sower and bread for the eater, so is my word that goes out from my mouth: it will not return to me empty, but will accomplish what I desire and achieve the purpose for which I sent it" (Isa. 55:10–11, NIV).

The Word of God is not just for the world in general. It is personal. It is for you and for your young child. His Word is a general truth, but it is also a personal truth to which you can cleave. Hide His Word in your heart, fully trusting in the fact His Word is for you and yours.

As you speak the Word of God over your child, let His will become your will. Believe for His absolute best for your child. Pray for His will to be done and His kingdom to come in the life of your little one and in your whole house. "And he said unto them, When ye pray, say, Our Father which art in heaven, hallowed by thy name. Thy kingdom come. Thy will be done, as in heaven, so in earth" (Luke 11:2, KJV).

Day 1

MORNING

Little one, our Father God will bless you that you might have confidence in Him and trust in His wondrous promises.

EVENING

______, God is always present to watch over you. He cares for the birds that fly, and you are more valuable to Him than many birds. He will take care of you.

Scripture Reading
Psalm 56:3, TLB
Matthew 10:29–31, TLB

MORNING

______, you are blessed with a calm and tranquil spirit because God is your strength. He is always present to help you.

EVENING

God has done amazing things for you, and you will not be afraid. God has blessed you with joy.

Scripture Reading
Isaiah 41:10, TLB
Joel 2:21

Day 3

MORNING

Our Lord is blessing you with boldness and strength. Fear and doubt shall be far from you because the Lord is always with you.

EVENING

I pray that the opinions of others will not discourage your development. The Lord will be with you and see you through.

Scripture Reading
Joshua 1:9
Jeremiah 1:8

Day 4

MORNING

______, Jehovah will take care of you, so you will not fear bad news nor live in dread of what may happen.

EVENING

Our heavenly Father has blessed you with His unconditional love; His perfect love turns fear out of doors and expels every trace of terror!

Scripture Reading
Psalm 112:7, TLB
1 John 4:18, AMP, NIV

Day 5

MORNING

The Lord is doing a brand-new thing, and I entrust your future to Him.

EVENING

I pray that the fragrance of the knowledge of Jesus Christ will flow through you to others.

Scripture Reading
Isaiah 43:18–19
2 Corinthians 2:14

Day 6

MORNING

May the Lord bless you with the desire to seek first the kingdom of God and His righteousness.

EVENING

I ask the Lord to bless you and surround you with favor as with a shield. May He give you favor in your relationships, family and friends, teachers and schoolmates, future marriage, ministry and career.

Scripture Reading
Matthew 6:25–33
Psalm 5:12, NKJV

Day 7

MORNING

I pray that you will yield yourself to our heavenly Father's plans for your life. You can do all things through Christ because He will be your strength.

EVENING

May God give you a willing and obedient heart that you may eat the good crops from the land.

Scripture Reading
Philippians 4:13
Isaiah 1:19, NCV

Day 8

MORNING

I pray that you will flourish like a stately tree. I thank God for helping you to bring forth good fruit.

EVENING

I pray that you will be rooted and grounded in love. May you bear godly fruit of love, joy, peace, patience, kindness, goodness, faithfulness, gentleness and self-control.

Scripture Reading
Psalm 92:12–15
Ephesians 3:17
Galatians 5:22

Day 9

MORNING

______, I thank God for flooding your mind with wisdom and creative ideas.

EVENING

______, you were created for His pleasure, and you will be transformed daily into the image and likeness of God's dear Son!

Scripture Reading
Proverbs 8:12

Day 10

MORNING

Whatever the Lord has planned for you to do, may you do it all for His glory!

EVENING

______, you did not choose the Father, but He has chosen you.

Scripture Reading
1 Corinthians 10:31, NIV
John 15:16, NKJV

Day 11

MORNING

I pray that you will bless others, keeping God's ways and doing what is right and just in His sight. I pray that your offspring will be a blessing to all the nations of the earth.

EVENING

As we say good night, I pray that you will live a life worthy of the calling you have received from the Lord.

Spiritual Reading
Genesis 22:17–18
Ephesians 4:1

MORNING

Father God will go before you and take care of everything you will need. His generosity exceeds even ours, in the glory that pours from Jesus.

EVENING

The Lord is your light and your salvation, and He will protect you from danger. With Him on your side, you are fearless, afraid of nothing and no one.

Scripture Reading
Philippians 4:19, The Message
Psalm 27:1, The Message, TLB

Day 13

MORNING

Little one, our God doesn't want you to be shy with His gifts, but bold, loving and sensible. We love our heavenly Father because He first loved us.

EVENING

It is our prayer that you will always seek the Lord. He will answer you, and He will deliver you from all your fears.

Scripture Reading
2 Timothy 1:7, The Message
Psalm 34:4, NIV

Day 14

MORNING

I pray that you will obey God's Word and guard His teachings as you would your own eyes. Remind yourself of them; write them on your heart as if on a tablet.

EVENING

I rejoice knowing that God has brought you into the kingdom of His dear Son.

Scripture Reading
Proverbs 7:2–3, NCV
Colossians 1:13, TLB

Day 15

MORNING

I thank God for the life-giving Spirit that makes you free to be the person He created you to be.

EVENING

May you always be content with who you are. Father God's strong hand is on you; He will promote you at the right time. I pray that you will live carefree before Him, because He is most careful with you.

Scripture Reading
Romans 8:2, TLB
1 Peter 5:6–7, The Message

Day 16

MORNING

It is so wonderful to know that the Lord is here with us as we begin our day. I pray that He will teach you His way and lead you in a plain path.

EVENING

______, I bind you to His mercy and look to Him for your protection.

Scripture Reading
Psalm 27:11
Psalm 56:1, TLB

Day 17

MORNING

I rejoice because the Lord will work out His plans for your life—for His loving-kindness continues forever. He will not abandon you—for He made you.

EVENING

______, even before you hear ungodly ideas, I use our powerful God-tools for smashing warped philosophies and tearing down barriers you might erect against the truth of God. I fit every loose thought, emotion and impulse into the structure of life shaped by Christ.

Scripture Reading

Psalm 138:8, TLB
2 Corinthians 10:5, THE MESSAGE

Day 18

MORNING

May you not just listen to His Word, but be obedient to its message so that you will not be self-deceived.

EVENING

May the Lord bless you to make wise choices.

Scripture Reading
James 1:22
Deuteronomy 30:19, TLB

Day 19

MORNING

I believe that you, ______, will choose to love the Lord, to obey Him and to cling to Him. You will then be able to live safely.

EVENING

I pray that you will always trust in Him. May you be kind and good to others; then you will live safely here in the land and prosper, feeding in safety.

Scripture Reading
Deuteronomy 30:20, TLB
Psalm 37:3, TLB

MORNING

I ask the Holy Spirit to reveal the truth to you; you shall know the truth, and the truth shall make you free to make wise choices.

EVENING

May you be quick to hear, slow to speak and slow to become angry.

Scripture Reading
John 8:32
James 1:19, NIV

Day 21

MORNING

I thank God that as I teach and train you up in the way that you are to go, you will receive Jesus as your personal Savior and come to know your heavenly Father.

EVENING

May you stretch out, reaching for the Lord, and never run out of good things to write or say.

Scripture Reading
Psalm 146:5, TLB
Psalm 71:14–15, THE MESSAGE

Day 22

MORNING

______, you are more than a conqueror through Christ Jesus who loves you!

EVENING

______, the power of life and death is in the tongue. I pray that your words will be filled with wisdom, for they will chart the course of your destiny.

Scripture Reading
Romans 8:37
Proverbs 18:21

Day 23

MORNING

I pray that you will know your God and that you shall be strong and do great things.

EVENING

______, the Lord your God teaches you what is best for you. He directs you in the way you should go. I thank Father God for His promises!

Scripture Reading
Daniel 11:32, TLB
Isaiah 48:17

Day 24

MORNING

For your daughter:
And now, my daughter, don't be afraid. Our God will do for you all that you ask. People shall know you as a woman of noble character.

For your son:
Son, the Lord is with you, and you shall be a mighty man of courage.

EVENING

______, I pray that your ways will be pleasing to the Lord. He will make even your enemies live at peace with you.

Scripture Reading
Ruth 3:11
Judges 6:12
Proverbs 16:7

Day 25

MORNING

I pray that you will trust in the Lord and be unmoved by any circumstance.

EVENING

Father God has been with you from birth and will help you constantly. I will always praise Him!

Scripture Reading
Psalm 125:1, NIV
Psalm 71:6, TLB

Day 26

MORNING

May the Lord bless you with a cheerful disposition. Your cheerful heart does good like a medicine.

EVENING

I bless you that you might press on toward the goal to win the prize for which God has called you heavenward in Christ Jesus.

Scripture Reading
Proverbs 17:22, The Message, TLB
Philippians 3:14, NIV

Day 27

MORNING

I ask that our Lord God will favor you and give you success. May He give permanence to all you do.

EVENING

I pray that you will let your good deeds glow for all to see, so that others will praise our heavenly Father.

Scripture Reading
Psalm 90:17, TLB
Matthew 5:16

Day 28

MORNING

Praise the Lord! You shall be honored everywhere, for good men's sons and daughters are blessed with a special heritage.

EVENING

I reverence God. He will teach us how to choose the best. We shall live within God's circle of blessing, and you, my child, shall inherit the earth.

Scripture Reading
Psalm 112:1–2, TLB
Psalm 25:12–13, TLB

Day 29

MORNING

I ask the Lord to direct our work in truth, and I thank Him for establishing His covenant with us. Our descendants will be known among the nations and our offspring among the peoples. All who see them will acknowledge that they are a people the Lord has blessed.

EVENING

As arrows are in the hand of a mighty man, so is the child of our youth. Holy Spirit, show me in which direction to point my child so that he or she may strike the devil and his regime long after we have departed from the earth.[7]

Scripture Reading
Isaiah 61:8–9, NIV
Psalm 127:4

Day 30

MORNING

______, I ask God to bless you with a will to obey your parents.

EVENING

May the Lord give you a heart to honor your father and mother. He will bless you with a long life, full of blessing.

Scripture Reading
Ephesians 6:1–3, TLB

Day 31

MORNING

Before the Lord our God, I purpose to be careful to obey all of His commandments. I receive His promise that if we do what is right in His eyes, all will go well with us and our children forever.

EVENING

I ask the Holy Spirit to show me things to come that I might train up and teach you, my child, to choose the right path. When you are older, you will remain upon it.

Scripture Reading

Deuteronomy 12:28, TLB
John 16:13
Proverbs 22:6, KJV, TLB

NOVEMBER

The Lord Is Always Present

November

CONFESSING THE POWERFUL TRUTH OF THE WORD OF GOD

The Word of God is not just words written on a page or an account of what God did in the past. His Word is so powerful and creative that the world was framed by it. "By faith we understand that the worlds were framed by the word of God, so that the things which are seen were not made of things which are visible" (Heb. 11:3, NKJV). The Word of God is creative in nature, and therefore it is still creating today.

You are using a very powerful weapon when you speak truth from the Word of God over your child. It is a quick, sharp and powerful weapon that divides light from dark. The Word of God is called a sword in Hebrews 4:12: "For the word of God is quick, and powerful, and sharper than any twoedged sword, piercing even to the dividing asunder of soul and spirit, and of the joints and marrow, and is a discerner ot the thoughts and intents of the heart" (KJV). In Revelation 1:16 Jesus Christ, the Son of man, is described as having a sharp, double-edged sword coming out of His mouth.

We are not speaking mere words when we speak forth the truth of the Word of God. When we speak in agreement with God's Word, our words are spirit and life. In John 6:63, Jesus said, "The Spirit gives life; the flesh counts for nothing. The words I have spoken to you are spirit and they are life" (NIV). When we speak the truth of the Bible, we are speaking the Word of God as revealed by His Son, Jesus Christ. His words become our words. Those words that we speak are therefore spirit and life.

His words that are being spoken through us are quick, powerful and sharper than any double-edged sword.

Further evidence of the creative power of the Word of God lies in the fact that we were born again by His truth. It was God's will for us to be spiritually born into His eternal kingdom and to reign with Him in truth and love. "Of his own will begat he us with the word of truth, that we should be a kind of firstfruits of his creatures" (James 1:18, KJV).

Jesus, the Lord and Savior we serve, is the Truth. "Jesus saith unto him, I am the way, the truth, and the life" (John 14:6, KJV). All authority of heaven and earth has been given to Jesus Christ, and you are a joint heir with Him. When you speak His Word of truth, your words carry the weight of the authority of His kingdom, His Word and His unchangeable promises.

God keeps His truth. It is forever (Ps. 146:6), abundant (Exod. 34:6), exhibited in His ways and His works (Rev. 15:3, Ps. 33:4), enduring to all generations (Ps. 100:5), the fulfillment of promises in Christ (2 Cor. 1:20), the fulfillment of His covenant (Mic. 7:20) and a shield and buckler to the saints (Ps. 91:4).

The word of truth that is near, in your mouth and in your heart, is powerful. As you agree with the truth of the Word of God and speak blessings over your child, you are speaking in Christ in the sight of God. He will watch over His Word, and He will perform it. His Word will never wither or fade away, God's Word is sure and stands forever. "The grass withers and the flowers fall, but the word of our God stands forever" (Isa. 40:8, NIV).

Day 1

MORNING

I ask God to guard you from every evil. He will guard you when you leave and when you return. He is guarding you now, and He will guard you always.

EVENING

This evening I thank the Lord for watching over you. The Lord will watch over your coming and going both now and forever.

Scripture Reading
Psalm 121:7–8, NIV, THE MESSAGE

MORNING

I thank Father God for going with you wherever you are today.

EVENING

I ask our holy Father to guard you as you pursue His life that He conferred as a gift through Jesus. I thank Him for posting a night watch about you this evening.

Scripture Reading
Genesis 28:15, NIV
John 17:11–20, The Message

Day 3

MORNING

______, God is your Guardian, and He is right at your side to protect you. He won't fall asleep, and He will keep you from stumbling.

EVENING

I thank Father God for your salvation.

Scripture Reading
Psalm 121:5, The Message
1 John 5:18, NKJV

Day 4

MORNING

God will keep your life, _____. He has written in the Bible so long ago many things that are to teach you patience and that will keep you encouraged.

EVENING

You, ______, are blessed because God's plans for you will stand forever. He will keep you.

Scripture Reading
Romans 15:4–5, TLB
Psalm 33:4–11, TLB

Day 5

MORNING

In the name of Jesus I bless you, ______, with the benefits He has bestowed on you. His plans are perfect, and in the fullness of time we will understand what eye has not seen and ear has not heard. He is keeping them ready for you.

EVENING

May the Lord help you to listen well to His Word. You will keep His message in plain view at all times, and you will concentrate so that you learn it by heart. ______, you will really live and burst with health!

Scripture Reading
1 Corinthians 2:9, AMP
Proverbs 4:20–22, The Message

MORNING

You are blessed with His promise that preserves your life. The Lord will bless your coming in and going out.

EVENING

I ask the Lord to bless you with His revelation that pulls your life together.

Scripture Reading
Psalm 121:7–8, NRSV
Psalm 119:50, NIV
Psalm 19:7–8, The Message

Day 7

MORNING

Before Almighty God and our Father, I bless you with His Word. It will keep you and make your life productive.

EVENING

Baby ______, you are blessed, for the Father God is always watching over you; He never sleeps. He cares for you, defends you and protects you day and night.

Scripture Reading
Isaiah 55:10–11, TLB
Psalm 121:4, TLB

Day 8

MORNING

______, I thank the everlasting Father for loving you even as He loves Jesus.

EVENING

All glory to God, who is able to keep you from stumbling. He will bring you into His glorious presence with great joy.

Scripture Reading
John 15:10–11, NIV
Jude 24–25, NLT

Day 9

MORNING

Precious one, you are most blessed. Wherever you walk, God's Word will guide you; whenever you rest, it will guard you.

EVENING

His blessings are upon you, and He will always hold you by the hand and guide you. You will tell the world what great things He does.

Scripture Reading
Proverbs 6:22–23, The Message
Psalm 73:23–24, NIV, The Message

Day 10

MORNING

I thank God for blessing you. I pray that when you don't know which way to turn, whether to the right or to the left, you will hear a voice saying, "This is the way; walk in it."

EVENING

The Father and I will teach you to ask for His wisdom when you don't know what to do. He gives generously to all without finding fault, and it will be given to you.

Scripture Reading
Isaiah 30:21, NIV
James 1:5, NIV

Day 11

MORNING

I pray that you will delight in the ways of our God, and then you will walk with firm steps. May God have a good grip on your hand.

EVENING

Mighty God will save you when you are in trouble. He is your light! He makes your darkness bright. By His power, you can crush an army, and by His strength, you can leap over a wall.

Scripture Reading
Psalm 37:23–24, NIV, THE MESSAGE
2 Samuel 22:28–30, TLB

Day 12

MORNING

May our God instruct you and teach you in the way you should go. I thank Him for loving you and counseling you with His eye upon you.

EVENING

______, the Most High God is your Rock and your Fortress. I ask Him to honor His name by leading you out of any danger.

Scripture Reading
Psalm 32:8, AMP
Psalm 31:3–6, TLB

Day 13

MORNING

Baby ______, the Lord will keep you. The eternal God is your refuge and dwelling place, and underneath you are the everlasting arms.

EVENING

I thank our Lord God for being a sun and shield. You have been blessed with His favor and honor. He is not withholding any good thing from you.

Scripture Reading
Psalm 121, NRSV
Deuteronomy 33:27, AMP
Psalm 84:11–12, NIV

Day 14

MORNING

I come with you, our little one, to the throne of our gracious God. There you will receive mercy and find grace to help you when you need it.

EVENING

I thank the Lord for keeping you when you are going out and when you are coming in. He gives rest to those He loves. My child, you are His best gift to me—His generous legacy.

Scripture Reading
Hebrews 4:16, TLB
Psalm 127:2–3, 5, The Message

Day 15

MORNING

I am comforted because the Lord has blessed you. He keeps you, and He will not slumber nor sleep. When you have tasks to do, you will not be alone. The Lord keeps you secure.

EVENING

May the Lord God keep you constantly renewed in the spirit of your mind (having a fresh mental and spiritual attitude). May you put on the new nature (the regenerate self) created in His image (be Godlike), in true righteousness and holiness.

Scripture Reading
Numbers 11:17
Ephesians 4:23–24, AMP

Day 16

MORNING

______, the Lord will keep you safe. God has blessed you to be a person of understanding who delights in wisdom.

EVENING

______, our God plans to prosper you and to give you hope and a future. When you pray to Him, He will listen to you.

Scripture Reading
Proverbs 10:23–25
Jeremiah 29:11–13, NIV

Day 17

MORNING

Baby ______, the God of hosts has blessed you to seek good, and He will be with you. The Lord God will keep your life.

EVENING

From this time on and forevermore God loves you and keeps you, ______.

Scripture Reading
Amos 5:14–15, AMP
Deuteronomy 7:9, AMP

Day 18

MORNING

______, I love our heavenly Father. We stay close to Him, and He takes care of us. I thank Him for blessing you with courage and strength.

EVENING

I thank our Father God for keeping us today. ______, God has blessed you by calling you into companionship and participation with His Son, Jesus Christ our Lord.

Scripture Reading
Psalm 31:23–24, The Message
1 Corinthians 1:9, AMP

Day 19

MORNING

_____, the Father God will bless you to be helpful and kind to others.

EVENING

From this time on and forevermore, He who keeps you will not slumber nor sleep. I thank Him for His faithfulness to you this evening.

Scripture Reading
Hebrews 10:23–24, TLB
Psalm 121, NRSV
Psalm 89:8, AMP

Day 20

MORNING

Little one, God has revealed His Word to us that we might obey it. He will keep us safe.

EVENING

Tonight I thank our Lord God for tending His flock like a shepherd. He gathers you in His arms and carries you close to His heart.

Scripture Reading
Deuteronomy 29:29, TLB
Isaiah 40:11, NIV

Day 21

MORNING

May God bless you so that you will love what is good. He will keep your life joyful.

EVENING

The Father God deserves our thanks. His love for you, ______, will never quit.

Scripture Reading
Psalm 45:7, TLB
Psalm 136:1, THE MESSAGE

Day 22

MORNING

The Lord will keep your going out and your coming in, ______. I proclaim that you will enjoy the fruits of your labors, for these are gifts from God.

EVENING

I ask the Good Shepherd to keep you this evening. No one can take you from out of His hand.

Scripture Reading
Psalm 121, NRSV
Ecclesiastes 3:12–14, TLB
John 10:28, THE MESSAGE

Day 23

MORNING

I praise our heavenly Father for choosing you, _____. He will lead you to look to His Son, and you will believe in Him. You shall have eternal life.

EVENING

I thank Father God for making provision for you. Baby, always believe in the Lord Jesus, and you will be saved—you and your household.

Scripture Reading
John 6:37–40, NIV
Acts 16:31, NIV

MORNING

I thank our heavenly Father for pouring out His love into you by the Holy Spirit.

EVENING

For God loved you, ______, so much that He gave His only Son so that when you believe in Him, you shall not perish but have eternal life.

Scripture Reading
Romans 5:5, NIV
John 3:16, TLB

Day 25

MORNING

I thank our mighty God that your feet are on the path of life, all radiant from the shining of His face. When you take His hand, you are on the right way.

EVENING

I thank our Everlasting Father that you keep His Word. Because you keep His Word in passionate patience, He will keep you safe in the times of testing. May you keep a tight grip on what you have so that no one distracts you.

Scripture Reading
Psalm 16:11, The Message
Revelation 3:10–11, The Message

Day 26

MORNING

May Father God bless you to stay in His refreshing presence. How refreshing it is! ______, you will grow up and tell the world what God does.

EVENING

______, you are blessed and can be sure of this: God is with you always, even to the end of the world.

Scripture Reading
Psalm 73:25–28, The Message
Matthew 28:20, TLB

MORNING

Father God has blessed you with His promise for salvation that preserves your life. Let the name of the Lord be praised, both now and forevermore.

EVENING

______, the Lord will keep your life. God is your refuge and strength. He is ever present.

Scripture Reading
Psalm 119:50, NIV
Psalm 113:2, NIV
Psalm 46:1–2, NIV

Day 28

MORNING

Father God has blessed you, ______, by choosing you and calling you to come to Him. He filled you with Christ's goodness, gave you right standing with Himself and promised you His glory. I thank the Lord for being on your side.

EVENING

The Lord God has said that He will cause all His goodness to pass in front of you, and He will proclaim His name, the Lord, so you can hear it. May the Lord have mercy and compassion on you this evening and forevermore.

Scripture Reading
Romans 8:30–31, TLB
Exodus 33:19, NIV

Day 29

MORNING

______, your times are in the Lord's hands. May He deliver you from your enemies and from those who pursue you. May His face shine on you, saving you in His unfailing love.

EVENING

What a great thing! ______, salvation and power are established in the kingdom of our God, the authority of our Messiah! Our accuser is thrown out. ______, you will defeat him through the blood of the Lamb and the bold word of your witness.

Scripture Reading
Psalm 31:15–16, NIV
Revelation 12:10–12, The Message

Day 30

MORNING

I thank the Lord for His goodness to you, His love that endures forever and His faithfulness that continues through all generations.

EVENING

I thank the Lord God of heaven, the great and awesome God, for keeping His covenant of unfailing love toward you, ______. His eyes are open to hear the prayer that His servants are praying before Him day and night. I thank Him for blessing your going out and your coming in.

Scripture Reading
Psalm 100:4–5, NIV
Nehemiah 1:5, NLT
Psalm 121, NRSV

DECEMBER

Knowing Jesus

December

REJOICE

It is God's will for your joy and your child's joy to be full. Many times we settle for a limited amount of joy because we have allowed ourselves to become accustomed to listening the voice of defeat and worry. The Word of God has been given to us so that our joy will be full. "And these things write we unto you, that your joy may be full" (1 John 1:4, KJV). Meditating on the Word of Truth, the goodness of God, His promises, His testimonies, His nature, His fullness, His authority and His love will bring untold joy in your life. The worries of this life will begin to drop off and be replaced with joy, confidence and faith when you put on the mind of Christ.

This is a wonderful time of celebration because we are rejoicing in God's gift to us, His Son Jesus Christ. His life on earth is our example. Because He knew no sin, He was the perfect offering for our sins. During His life on earth, He only did what He saw His Father in heaven doing. His will was completely bound to the will of God. His love for us was overflowing, while at the same time His eyes were fixed on heaven and the purpose He was sent forth to do.

Keep in mind and close to your heart that God's love for you and for your little one has no boundaries. "And I pray that you, being rooted and established in love, may have power, together with all the saints, to grasp how wide and long and high and deep is the love of Christ, and to know this love that surpasses knowledge—that you may be filled to the measure of all the fullness of God" (Eph. 3:17–19, NIV).

It is impossible for you to comprehend how wide, how long, how high and how deep His love is for you and your baby. When the Father God looks at you, He sees the life of His Son because we are alive and made new creatures in Him. God the Father loved you so much that He gave His own Son for you. He bruised His own Son for you. "Yet it pleased the LORD to bruise Him; He has put Him to grief" (Isa. 53:10, NKJV).

God bruised His Son for you because your redemption and fullness of joy is His will for you. Jesus came to earth as a gift to you, and even though He was completely sinless, He was made sin for you so that in Him you could become the righteousness of God. "For He made Him who knew no sin to be sin for us, that we might become the righteousness of God in Him" (2 Cor. 5:21, NKJV).

Jesus came so that you and your child could have abundant, eternal life. Never question God's love for you. All of His promises are fulfilled in Christ Jesus. Because of Him, all of His promises are "yes and amen" to you. This is the reason why He gave Himself as a sacrifice for you. Even during times of sorrow and tribulation, there is reason to rejoice. If you are living in Him, you are fellowshiping with His sufferings during times of trial and persecution. This intimate fellowship with His sufferings is actually a time to rejoice and be glad about all He has done and all He is about to do.

Let the bells of your heart rejoice. Let the trumpet of your voice announce His praises. Open wide your mouth to shout and sing the truth of His Word. And let the tenderness of your arms embrace your little one as you declare the truth of His Word that reigns forevermore!

Day 1

MORNING

I thank our heavenly Father for loving you so much that He gave you Jesus. Jesus is your Wonderful Counselor, Mighty God, Everlasting Father and Prince of Peace.

EVENING

I exalt the Lord our God and praise His name, for He has done wonderful things in our lives today. I know that you, ______, are among the purposes planned of old (and fulfilled) in faithfulness and truth. I exalt Him, King Jesus.

Scripture Reading
Isaiah 9:6–7, AMP
Isaiah 25:1, AMP

Day 2

MORNING

Little one, our Wonderful Counselor has blessed us with good tidings for this day. We will lift up our voices with strength and stand unafraid as we behold our God. I thank Him for our rewards in Christ Jesus.

EVENING

This day our mighty God has fed us like a good shepherd. I thank Him for keeping us. He has gathered us in His arms and carried us in His bosom. We feel safe as He gently leads those of us who have young children.

Scripture Reading
Isaiah 40:9–10, AMP

Day 3

MORNING

Jesus said, "All authority has been given to Me in heaven and on earth." Now I pray that you, my child, will be a true disciple of Jesus, and make disciples of all nations. Jesus promised to be with you always, even to the end of the age.

EVENING

"Glory to God in the heavenly heights, peace to all men and women on earth who please You." Just as Mary did, I will treasure the things God reveals to me about your future and think about them. May you be an imitator of the One who loves you.

Scripture Reading
Matthew 28:18–19, NIV
Luke 2:6–24, NCV, THE MESSAGE

Day 4

MORNING

When Jesus lived on earth His heavenly Father kept watch over His heart, for therein lie the wellsprings of life. He is our example, and I pray that you, ______, will be a true disciple of Jesus.

EVENING

You belong to God, and you are an heir with Christ. I thank Him for choosing you that you may set forth the wonderful deeds and display the virtues and perfections of Him who called us out of darkness into His marvelous light.

Scripture Reading
Proverbs 4:23
Romans 8:17, AMP
1 Peter 2:9, AMP

Day 5

MORNING

This morning I acknowledge the kingship of Jesus and His sovereignty. I pray that you, ______, will know who you are—a son (or daughter) of God created for His pleasure.

EVENING

I bless you to be an imitator of Jesus. You will follow me as I follow Jesus. My prayer is that you will always do what pleases God.

Scripture Reading
1 Corinthians 15:25–28
John 8:29

MORNING

I pray for our heavenly Father to help me teach you to speak blessings and clothe yourself in the wardrobe God picked out for you.

EVENING

I come with you, my child, acknowledging that our heavenly Father's throne is forever and ever. He loves righteousness, and He has anointed you with the oil of gladness.

Scripture Reading

James 3
Colossians 3, The Message
Hebrews 1:8–9, amp
Psalm 45:6–7

Day 7

MORNING

Listen, my child; I read to you the message God sent, the good news of peace through Jesus Christ, who is Lord of all. Jesus is anointed with the Holy Spirit and power, leaving us as witnesses of His good deeds.

EVENING

I pray to our Father in heaven that you will have the compassion of Jesus. May you be moved by compassion and bless others.

Scripture Reading
Acts 10:36–43, AMP
Mark 6:34

Day 8

MORNING

I pray that you will be clothed in kindness. As an imitator of Christ, you will be gracious and merciful, slow to anger and abundant in kindness.

EVENING

Just as Jesus humbled Himself and became obedient to His will, I pray that you, ______, will be under older people who love and care for you.

Scripture Reading
Nehemiah 9:17, NKJV
Philippians 2:8
1 Peter 5:5, NCV

Day 9

MORNING

Unto us was born a Savior, a Wonderful Counselor, a Mighty God, an Everlasting Father and a Prince of Peace. I receive Jesus, and I purpose to lead you, ______, according to His example. He gave you the right to become a child of God.

EVENING

Blessed is ______. You will come to know that your strength is in God our Savior. You shall go from strength to strength, clothed in quiet strength.

Scripture Reading
Isaiah 9:6, 12, KJV
Psalm 84:5, 7, NKJV

Day 10

MORNING

I pray that when you are older, you will believe that Jesus is the Messiah. For to us, certainly a Child has been born, and this Child is Jesus. The eternal life that God has given to us is in the Son, and whoever believes in the Son has life.

EVENING

It is good to give thanks to the Lord. I bring you before our heavenly Father, rejoicing and singing praises to His name. ______, you will declare His loving-kindness in the morning and His faithfulness every night.

Scripture Reading

1 John 5, AMP
Psalm 92: 1–2, NIV

Day 11

MORNING

I thank God for loving us. I pray that His joy and delight will be in you, complete and overflowing. May you love Him with all your heart and love others as He has loved you.

EVENING

I thank Father God that He is making known to you the path of life. This is a life filled with joy in His presence, with eternal pleasures at every turn. You shall call Him the Everlasting Father and the Prince of Peace.

Scripture Reading
John 15:11–12, AMP
Psalm 16:11, NIV

Day 12

MORNING

Before the Lord, I bless you, my child, today with a promise from Him that there is hope in this world. I thank Him for the riches of the glory of the mystery, which is Christ within and among us, the hope of [realizing the] glory.

EVENING

I ask the Holy Spirit to help me teach you to seek God's approval rather than man's. May you always walk in harmony with His will and may you be at peace.

Scripture Reading
Colossians 1:27, AMP
John 12:42–43

Day 13

MORNING

______, rest assured that you can take courage when you hold on to God's promise with confidence. This confidence is like a strong and trustworthy anchor for your soul.

EVENING

This evening I thank our heavenly Father for the Child that He gave to the world. Today we live by faith in the Son of God.

Scripture Reading
Hebrews 6:18–19
Galatians 2:20, NIV

Day 14

MORNING

I thank our Lord God that you will seriously live the new resurrection life with Christ. May you pursue Christlike things and see things from His perspective. Jesus is our new life in God.

EVENING

______, you are God's workmanship, created in Christ Jesus to do good works. God has prepared projects in advance for you to do. You will do all these as unto the Lord.

Scripture Reading
Colossians 3:1–4, The Message
Ephesians 2:10, NIV

Day 15

MORNING

______, you are justified through faith and have peace with God through Jesus. Jesus is the Prince of Peace, and we rejoice in the hope of the glory of God.

EVENING

I pray that the God who gives hope will fill you, ______, with much joy and peace while you trust in Him. Then your hope will overflow by the power of the Holy Spirit. I thank Father God for His Son, born to us for our salvation.

Scripture Reading
Romans 5: 1–2, NIV
Romans 15:13, NCV

Day 16

MORNING

I pray that you will walk as Jesus walked. May you clothe yourself with humility, for He gives grace to the humble. I pray that you will walk in self-confidence because Jesus is your Lord.

EVENING

May you live for the glory of God in Christ Jesus.

Scripture Reading
Colossians 3:12
Romans 6:11

Day 17

MORNING

I ask that the God of our Lord Jesus Christ, the glorious Father, give to you the Spirit of wisdom and revelation.

EVENING

Little one, I pray that whatever you do or say, it will be as a representative of the Lord Jesus, and together we will give thanks through Him to God the Father.

Scripture Reading
Ephesians 1:17–18, NIV
Colossians 3:17, NLT

Day 18

MORNING

______, our heavenly Father knew you before He made the world, and He decided that you would be like His Son.

EVENING

______, the Spirit Himself joins with our spirits to say we are God's children. We receive blessings from God together with Christ.

Scripture Reading
Romans 8:29, NCV
Romans 8:16–17, NCV

Day 19

MORNING

This morning I just want to thank our Everlasting Father. He has given us the victory through our Lord Jesus Christ. I thank Him for the marvelous changes in our lives.

EVENING

Our Everlasting Father, Almighty God, has made you more than a conqueror in Christ Jesus. I thank Him for His watchful eye over you. His love abounds more and more in you.

Scripture Reading
1 Corinthians 15:57, NIV
Romans 8:37, NIV

Day 20

MORNING

He has been called Wonderful Counselor, Mighty God, Everlasting Father, the Prince of Peace. This morning I bless you, my child, because Jesus has enriched you in every way—in all your speaking and in all your knowledge.

EVENING

As we rest tonight, we will glory in the Lord's love. I thank Him that through His Holy Spirit and by faith we have strength and power in our inner beings. We are learning of the height and depth of His great love for us.

Scripture Reading
1 Corinthians 1:5, NIV
Ephesians 3:16–19, NIV

Day 21

MORNING

Our heavenly Father predestined you to be adopted as His son (or daughter) through Jesus Christ. He finds pleasure in this relationship.

EVENING

______, you are blessed with a strong heart that is full of courage and tenacity. Though outwardly we are wasting away, inwardly we are yet being renewed every day. I will train you up in the Word of God so that you will keep your direction toward the final goal.

Scripture Reading
Ephesians 1:5–6, NIV
2 Corinthians 4:16, NIV

Day 22

MORNING

I bless you daily with the food of faith and love. May you be filled with hope for the word of truth, for the gospel is your mainstay. The Prince of Peace is your companion and strength for this day.

EVENING

We are secure, for we have received God's abundant provision of grace and the gift of righteousness through Jesus Christ. We rest in perfect peace tonight, consoled by thoughts of His love for us.

Scripture Reading
Colossians 1:5, NIV
Romans 5:17, NIV

Day 23

MORNING

______, I thank Almighty God that you will find salvation in the Son that He has given us. I will teach you that there is no other name under heaven given to men by which we must be saved.

EVENING

I purpose to teach you, my child ______, in a spirit of profound common sense so that I can begin to bring you to maturity. I pray that you will use the divine energy God generously gives you to do your very best.

Scripture Reading
Acts 4:12, NIV
Colossians 1:28, The Message

Day 24

MORNING

I thank God for this beautiful Christmas Eve. I rejoice that our heavenly Father gave us His Son, Jesus. I thank Jesus for bearing our sins on the cross so that we could live unto righteousness. By His stripes we were healed.

EVENING

Before Father God, this evening we are so aware that we need Jesus. We go to bed with great expectation, for tomorrow is Jesus' birthday. We are thankful for His compassion for us. It is so great. He has cast all our sins into the depths of the sea.

Scripture Reading
1 Peter 2:24, KJV
2 Corinthians 5:17, KJV

Day 25

MORNING

______, we are passing on to you our tradition of celebrating Christmas, the day chosen to honor our Lord's birth. We pray that you will follow in our footsteps and set aside this time as holy. Jesus is the Word that came to earth and lived among us. In the beginning He was with God, and He was God. He is full of grace and truth, and from Him we receive one gift after another. We give Jesus all that we have—we give Him ourselves.

EVENING

We pray that you will learn to meditate on God's Son and His kingdom. He is our great High Priest who has gone through the heavens on our behalf. Let us always hold firmly to this faith I profess.

Scripture Reading
John 1:1, 14–16, NCV
Hebrews 4:14, NIV

Day 26

MORNING

_____, together we thank Father God for the birth of His Son. His name is Jesus—"God saves"—because He will save His people from their sins. He is also called "Emmanuel," which is Hebrew for "God is with us."

EVENING

_____, I pray and believe that you will receive the Gift that the Father God has given you: Jesus is His name.

Scripture Reading
Matthew 1:21, KJV, THE MESSAGE
John 1:12

Day 27

MORNING

______, we pray that you will inherit our desire to be a vessel of honor to glorify our God. I know that whatever I ask in Jesus' name, He will do. I ask for His will be done in our lives today.

EVENING

______, may you inherit a willingness to be in agreement with your godly parents and caregivers. In the name of our Lord Jesus Christ, I pray that we will be completely joined together by having the same kind of thinking and the same purpose. I bind our minds to the mind of Christ that we may hold the thoughts, feelings and purposes of His heart.

Scripture Reading
John 14:13–14, KJV
1 Corinthians 1:10, NCV
1 Corinthians 2:16, AMP

Day 28

MORNING

______, you are blessed, for Father God is always with you. Whatever you do in word or deed, do it all in the name of Jesus, giving thanks to God and the Father by Him.

EVENING

______, always remember that Almighty God's law is perfect and restores the whole person. May your actions be filled with the knowledge that Jesus Christ is glorified, according to the grace of God.

Scripture Reading
Colossians 3:17, KJV
2 Thessalonians 1:12, KJV
Psalm 19:7, AMP

Day 29

MORNING

This morning I praise God for directing your life. I offer the sacrifice of praise to God continually. I thank God for making you a part of His kingdom and helping you to know the importance of being in it.

EVENING

I thank the Prince of Peace for being with you today. I thank Him for the reality of knowing that He loves you, ______, and that you will know that you are loved. May you be secure in the blessings of His love, believing that Jesus is the Christ, and may you share this godly love with others.

Scripture Reading
Hebrews 13:15, KJV
1 John 3:23, KJV

Day 30

MORNING

Our precious child, I thank God that Jesus is your example. You will be blessed as you grow in wisdom and in stature. Just as Jesus did, you will grow in favor with God and men. Jesus is our Wonderful Counselor, the Mighty God, the Everlasting Father, the Prince of Peace.

EVENING

I pray that you will inherit a joyous spirit. You will sing God's praises and enjoy the happiness of being one of His children. He mades the joy in you complete.

Scripture Reading
Luke 2:52
Psalm 9:2
John 15:11, NIV

Day 31

MORNING

______, I pray that you will rejoice in God our Savior. His name is majestic in all the earth!

EVENING

______, I thank God that you are of one heart and one mind with Him. You are learning to believe that Jesus was sent by God to save the world. I bless you with His love for you.

Scripture Reading
Isaiah 9:6
Psalm 8:1
John 17:21–23, The Message

NOTES

1. Adapted from Numbers 13:30 prayer, *Women of Destiny Bible,* ed. Cindy Jacobs (Nashville: Thomas Nelson Publishers, Inc., 2000), 164.

2. Adapted from 1 Samuel 15:22 prayer, *Women of Destiny Bible,* 323.

3. Adapted from 2 Samuel 7:22 prayer, *Women of Destiny Bible,* 351.

4. Adapted from 1 Kings 5:4 prayer, *Women of Destiny Bible,* 383.

5. Adapted from Esther 4:14 prayer, *Women of Destiny Bible,* 560.

6. Adapted from *The Life Recovery Bible* (Wheaton, IL: Tyndale House Publishers, Inc., 1998), 3.

7. David and Roxanne Swann, *Guarantee His Child's Success* (Tulsa, OK: Harrison House, 1990).

Use this page to write
your own special blessing for your child.

Use this page to write
your own special blessing for your child.

Use this page to write
your own special blessing for your child.

Use this page to write
your own special blessing for your child.

Use this page to write
your own special blessing for your child.

Use this page to write
your own special blessing for your child.

Use this page to write
your own special blessing for your child.

Use this page to write
your own special blessing for your child.